Paris
[1001]
[photos]

© 2008 Éditions Solar, an imprint of Place des Éditeurs
© 2009 Rebo International, b.v., Lisse, Netherlands

Text: Corinne Targat
Graphic Design: Gwénaël Le Cossec
Layout: Jacqueline Leymarie
Editorial Coordinator: Matthieu Sublet
Production: Thomas Lemaître
Photography: Frédéric Bar
Translation: Matthew Clarke for First Edition Translations Ltd, Cambridge, UK
Editor: David Price for First Edition Translations Ltd
Typesetting: Garamond Studio, Prague, Czech Republic
Copy Editor: Elizabeth A. Haas

ISBN: 978 90 366 2507 4

Paris
[1001]
[photos]

REBO
PUBLISHERS

Contents

Eternal Paris

Medieval Paris	8
Monuments and Men	40
Arts and Letters	70
Squares and Avenues	110
Paris in the 1900s: A Renaissance	126

Riverside Paris

And the Seine Runs Right Through the Center	156
From Bridge to Bridge	170
The Charm of the Canals	194
Fountains: The Living Springs of Paris	206

Exotic and Offbeat Paris

Paris: Showcase of the World	224
Secret Courtyards and Passages	236
Fabulous Beasts and Curious Decorations	256
Cemeteries and Catacombs	268

Natural Paris

Village Paris

Modern Paris

A Stroll in the Woods   286
Haussmann's Parks   294
Historical Gardens   306
Squares and Gardens   322

Montmartre: Bohemian   336
    Playground
From Belleville   348
    to Ménilmontant:
    The "Rebellious Children"
The Île Saint-Louis   358
    and the Île de la Cité:
    The Heart of the World
From Saint-Germain-des-Prés
    to the Latin Quarter: 368
    The Spirit of the Left Bank
La Butte-aux-Cailles: 376
    A Breath of Freedom
Montparnasse: 384
    The Crazy Years

The Trailblazers   394
    of Today's Paris
From Le Corbusier   416
    to Jean Nouvel
Paris in Motion   434
Fashion, Luxury, and Design   446

Index   458

Eternal Paris

The medieval beauty and glory of Paris was all but forgotten over the centuries until revived by the creative genius of Victor Hugo in 1831. His famous novel The Hunchback of Notre Dame definitively located the heart of medieval Paris within the triangle formed by Notre Dame Cathedral, the Louvre (once a fortress), and the Sainte-Chapelle (built by Saint Louis).

Medieval Paris

Though the restoration work of architect Viollet-le-Duc may have altered the look of the cathedral's fantastic creatures, the authentic spirit of the Middle Ages still lives here today.

Lutetia, a Gallo-Roman city on the Left Bank that can be glimpsed today in the old arenas and thermal baths of Cluny, was a forerunner of medieval Paris. Eventually the new city extended across the Cité (today the Latin Quarter) and the Seine, from the Jean-sans-Peur Tower to the Vincennes Château. The medieval era is evidenced not only by the splendid religious and military buildings here, but also the sumptuous civil architecture of the Hôtel de Sens and the Hôtel de Cluny. The latter, now the National Museum of the Middle Ages, used the foundations of Lutetia's ancient public baths, while heralding the more modern architectural style of the Parisian mansion—complete with a courtyard and garden—that sprang up during the 16th to the 18th century.

[1] The Neolithic canoes unearthed in 1997 during construction work in Bercy are now on display in the Carnavelet Museum.

[2], [3] and [4] Lutetia's arenas, built in the 1st century, were uncovered in 1869 by excavations undertaken to make way for Rue Monge.

C'EST ICI QU'A PRIS NAISSANCE AU DEUXIEME SIECLE DE NOTRE ERE LA VIE MUNICIPALE DE PARIS. DIX MILLE HOMMES POUVAIENT TENIR A L'AISE DANS LES

ARENES DE LUTECE

OU LES JOUTES NAUTIQUES SUCCEDAIENT AUX LUTTES DE GLADIATEURS. LES COMBATS DE FAUVES A LA RE-PRESENTATION DES COMEDIES ET DES DRAMES.

PASSANT SONGE DEVANT CE PREMIER MONUMENT DE PARIS QUE LA VILLE DU PASSE EST AUSSI LA CITE DE L'AVENIR ET CELLE DE TES ESPOIRS.

DON du SYNDICAT d'INITIATIVES des ARENES de LUTECE à l'OCCASION du Bi-MILLENAIRE de PARIS 1951
TEXTE de JEAN PAULHAN

[5] Only one third of Cluny's thermal baths survived the pillage of the Barbarians in the last days of the Roman Empire.

The Hôtel de Sens, which now houses the Forney Library, was one of the city's most opulent medieval residences.

[1] The main courtyard in the
Hôtel de Cluny, with its tower
and windows emblazoned
with heraldic motifs.
[2] This ornately decorated
staircase in the Hôtel de Cluny
leads to the medieval garden.

13

[1] Only the tower of the Saint-Jacques Church escaped demolition in 1802. It now serves as a meteorological station. [2] and [3] The Jean-sans-Peur Tower is the last surviving relic of the Hôtel de Bourgogne. The vault over its staircase is decorated with magnificent natural motifs.

[Left] The entrance is the only original part of the Hôtel de Clisson, although the building still has a medieval air.

[1] The majestic twin towers of Notre Dame, visible from the bridge, offer a breathtaking vantage point for viewing the city.

[2] The forecourt is not only a major tourist attraction but also marks mile zero for France's highways.
[3] The crypt displays the remains of the foundations of both the original building and the surrounding houses.

[4] The gargoyles on Rue du Cloître-Notre-Dame divert rainwater from the building's north side, but those on the façade are purely decorative.
[5] A stunning view of the south side from the Montebello embankment, now a departure point for tourist boats.

[1] The south rose window ("the midday rose") was donated by Saint Louis.
[2] The choir in Notre Dame still displays relics of the renovation undertaken by Louis XIII in 1638, such as the stalls and the Pietà by Guillaume Coustou.

[3] A magical lighting effect on the pillars in the nave of Notre Dame.
[4] Detail of the central doorway on the façade, showing the Last Judgment.
[5] The bas-reliefs on the choir date from the 14th century but were restored by Viollet-le-Duc in the 19th century. They illustrate the life of Christ.

19

[1] to [5] Viollet-le-Duc added monsters and demons near the rose window, thereby reinterpreting medieval fantasy for the 19th century.

[6] The Emmanuel bell was installed in 1686. Its clapper weighs 1,100 lb. (500 kg), and the whole bell some 13 tons. In the popular imagination, it is inextricably linked with Victor Hugo's Quasimodo.

[1] The doorway to the cloister, sculpted around 1250.
[2] Strolling along the Quai de la Tournelle.

[3] The Fountain of the Virgin, a neo-Gothic monument near the cathedral's apse in the Jean XXIII square.

[Right] The central rose window and the gallery of the Kings of Judah, which were destroyed by the revolutionaries (who mistook them for French kings!).

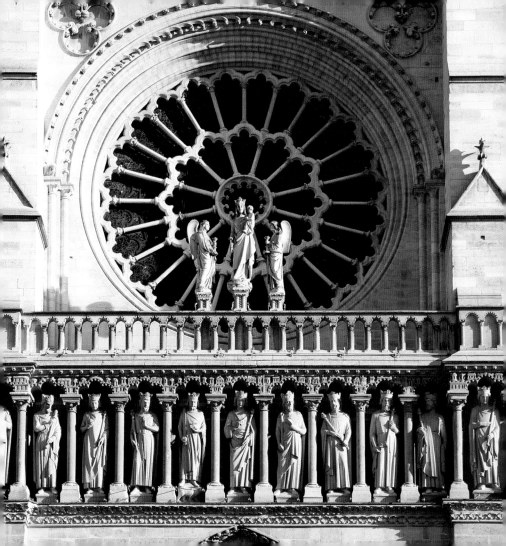

[1] The center of the vault in the porch of Saint-Germain-l'Auxerrois depicts the Last Supper. [2] The belfry next to Saint-Germain-l'Auxerrois dates from the 19th century. It looms over the local district's municipal headquarters.

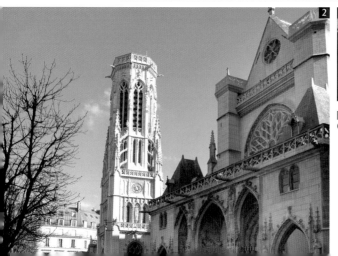

[3] Detail of the porch, showing Saint Genevieve resisting a devil.

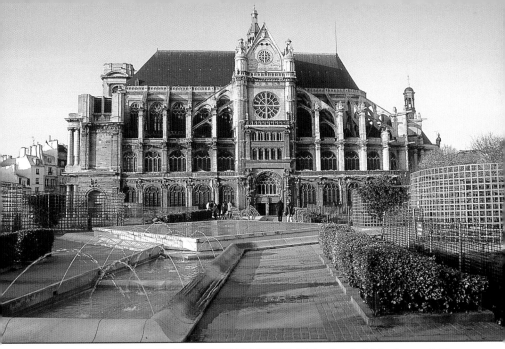

[4] The Church of Saint Eustace, built between 1532 and 1640, is a superb synthesis of the transition from the Gothic to the Renaissance. Its proportions echo those of Notre Dame.

[5] Relic of the original church founded in 1213 by the merchant Jean Alais in gratitude for his good fortune (the King decreed that he should receive a tax from every fish sold in Les Halles market, known as "Paris's stomach").

[1] Floral and animal motifs are still visible on the floor tiles in the central aisle of the upper chapel in the Sainte-Chapelle.
[2] The statues leaning against each pillar inside the Sainte-Chapelle depict the Twelve Apostles, each bearing one of the ritual crosses associated with the consecration of the church.
[3] The lower chapel is decorated with colorful paintwork that extends right up to the vault adorned with *fleurs de lys*, the symbol of the French monarchy.

[Right] Detail of the choir in the lower chapel.

[1] Five spires have been added to the Sainte-Chapelle since its construction. This one is made of cedar wood and is 108 ft. (33 m) high; it was built by Jean-Baptiste Lassus in 1853.
[2] This majestic stained-glass window in the upper chapel is made up of 1,113 pieces.

[3] The tympanum in the upper chapel in the Sainte-Chapelle portrays the Last Judgment.
[4] The Des Billettes cloister on Rue des Archives (no. 22) dates from 1427. It is now used for concerts and exhibitions.
[5] The original church in Saint-Germain-des-Prés harks back to the apogee of the Merovingian era in the 6th century. Its spire was added in the 19th century.

[1] The recently restored dungeon in Vincennes Château is a masterpiece of 14th-century military architecture (1337).
[2] The royal chapel in the castle's courtyard is an exuberant demonstration of the Gothic aesthetic.

[Following pages] The Quai de Gesvres offers a view of the Pont au Change, with the Conciergerie in the background.

[3] Portion of the boundary wall built by Philip Augustus, now preserved on Rue Clovis.
[4] The city wall runs for almost 90 yards (80 m) alongside the Charlemagne Lycée on Rue des Jardins-Saint-Paul.

31

[1] The magnificent hall of the Gens des Armes in the Conciergerie is a sumptuous architectural display, divided into four rows that together encompass a space of 19,000 sq. ft (1,800 sq. m.)
[2] The Cour des Femmes (Courtyard of Women).

[3] The capital on the central pillar in the Salle des Gardes depicts Abelard and Heloise.
[4] The square Clock Tower and the Caesar and Silver Towers. To the rear, the Bonbec Tower, which once housed a torture chamber notorious for its success in making victims talk.
[5] In 1585 this clock designed by Germaine Pilon replaced the country's first public clock.

35

The house of the alchemist Nicolas Flamel at no. 51, Rue de Montmorency. Built in 1407, it is the oldest house in Paris.

The house's recent restoration has spruced up its inscriptions and engraved images.

[1] and [2] The Rue de Bièvre owes its name to the river that once passed through the center of Paris. The remains of its medieval houses take visitors on a trip back in time.

[3] and [4] The corbelled houses on Rue du Grenier-sur-l'Eau mark the way to the heart of the medieval Marais.
[5] The houses at nos. 11 and 13 on Rue François-Miron are medieval but their timber framework was replaced as part of a renovation carried out in 1967.

The Panthéon was originally a religious building but in 1885 it became a temple extolling the glory of France's great and good.

From the City Hall to the Panthéon, from the Sorbonne to the Arc de Triomphe, Paris has witnessed twenty centuries of history, marked by architectural developments that exude passion and a thirst for innovation.

Everyday life on Paris's streets, avenues, and alleys has always been conducted against a backdrop of great, long-lasting historical monuments. Both middle- and working-class neighborhoods boast buildings that are every bit as impressive as the city's churches and palaces. This enchanting harmony, orchestrated by time itself, makes Paris the world's most beautiful city, guaranteed to delight. Its heritage is a gift to the world, waiting to be discovered by successive generations of visitors.

The visual treats on offer include the imposing façades of the ministries in Saint-Germain, the courtyards in the Hôtel de Soubise, the arcades and gilt adornments of the Invalides, the roofs of the Royal Palace, and the dome of the Panthéon.

The Napoleonic period and Haussmann's planning revolution transformed the layout of Paris by opening up spaces in front of old buildings and creating spectacular new ones. Narrow, winding medieval streets, with their hidden architectural treasures replete with history, rub shoulders with the major thoroughfares that opened the city up to the outside world and acted as showcases for its monuments.

The City Hall lost its Place de Grève to make way for a huge esplanade, while the

Monuments and Men

ancestral "triumphal way," leading from the Louvre toward the site of the Défense arch, was embellished by the Arc de Triomphe du Carrousel. The history of Paris has been played out among this extraordinary diversity and wonderful homogeneity.

[1] More than 20 lb. (10 kg) of gold leaf adorn the dome of the Invalides.
[2] and [3] Detail of a pediment in the main court-yard and a view of the church from the Place de Fontenoy.

[4] The Museum of Architectural Models, founded in 1777, was joined by the Artillery Museum in 1871 and the Army Museum in 1896.
[5] Sundial in the main courtyard.

[1] Various cannons from different periods are on display in the galleries and main courtyards of the Invalides, illustrating the development of military technology. The historical Army Museum was created in 1896 to chronicle the country's military traditions.

[1] The view from the south of the square highlights the Greek-cross layout of the Panthéon drawn up by Soufflot.
[2] and [3] The triangular pediment designed by David d'Angers, with the motto reading *To Great Men to Whom the Country is Grateful*, which was added in 1791.

[4] Foucault's pendulum was an experiment conceived to prove the rotation of the Earth. It was suspended from the vault of the Panthéon for its first public demonstration in 1851.

[5] The majesty of the dome, soaring to a height of 272 ft. (83 m), can be fully appreciated from Rue Soufflot.

[1] The rood loft in the Church of Saint-Étienne-du-Mont, built around 1530, is one of the most beautiful in all of Paris.
[2] Saint-Séverin is the oldest church on the Left Bank.
[3] The Church of Saint-Sulpice, made famous by *The Da Vinci Code* book, has been rebuilt several times. Six different architects took on the job in a period of 134 years.

[4] and [5] The Madeleine Church is surrounded by a peristyle with fifty-two columns. Its construction took eighty-five years to com-plete because it was interrupted by the political upheavals of the late 18th century.
[Following pages] The ornamental ponds in the Place Joffre, at the end of the Champ-de-Mars, set off the central pavilion of the Military School.

49

[1] In the Place du Palais-Bourbon, the sculptor Jean-Jacques Feuchière's statue of *The Law* watches sternly over the debates held inside the National Assembly.
[2] A legendary address: no. 36, Quai des Orfèvres—the police headquarters.

3

4

[3] La Cour du Mai flanked by the Sainte-Chapelle and the façade of the Palais de Justice.
[4] The City Hall is a neo-Renaissance pastiche, built in 1871 from plans drawn up in the 16th century.

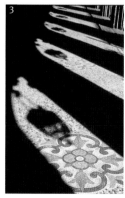

[1] The Place du Palais Royal, opposite the entrance to the Council of State.
[2] A series of elegant columns line the Orléans Gallery, which was once covered by a stained-glass window.
[3] The Montpensier Gallery, whose gracious arcade has witnessed much licentious behavior in its time!

5 [4] The courtyard in front of the Ministry of Culture, which stands opposite the Council of the Constitution.
[5] The *Café de Chartres* was the first restaurant in the modern sense of the term. It was rechristened the *Véfour* in 1820.

The Brongniart Palace is no longer home to the Stock Exchange as trading was computerized in 1987, but the majestic building is used for receptions and prestigious events.

The old corn exchange on the Rue des Viarmes began use as a commercial exchange in 1889. The four columns in the portico support a pediment crowned by three figures representing the City of Paris flanked by Abundance and Trade.

The Pavillon de l'Arsenal at no. 21, Boulevard Morland was built in 1876 to house private collections. Since 1987 it has put on exhibitions organized by the city of Paris. A statue paying homage to the poet Rimbaud ("the man with the wind at his heels") stands in front of the entrance.

1

[1] The Economic and Social Council on the Place d'Iéna, built between 1936 and 1946, was originally designed by Auguste Pernet to house the Museum of Public Works.

2

3

[2] and [3] The Gobelins workshop, closely associated with the politician Jean-Baptiste Colbert, was responsible for making precious objects for the Crown.

59

[1] The Hôtel de Rohan on Rue Vieille-du-Temple was drawn up by the architect Pierre-Alexis Delamair in 1705 for the Rohan family. Like the Hôtel de Soubise, it now houses part of the French national archives.

[2] *The Horses of the Sun* by Robert Le Lorrain was a stylish adornment to this mansion's former stables.

[3] The Hôtel Scipion Sardini, built in 1565, is the only mansion dating from the Middle Ages. It is also remarkable for its terracotta medallions.

[4] and [5] The Hôtel de Lassay, the official residence of the President of the National Assembly, reflects the high status of this post.

61

[1] and [2] The Hôtel de Noirmoutier, one of the most beautiful in Saint-Germain, is lined with wood trim evoking the fables of La Fontaine.

[Right] The gardens of the Hôtel Donon on Rue Payenne. The building now plays host to the Cognacq-Jay Museum.

[3] The Palace and Museum of the Légion d'Honneur are situated under the dome of the Hôtel de Saim on the Quai Anatole-France.

[1] The Hôtel de Soubise, at no. 60, Rue des Francs-Bourgeois, houses the Museum of the History of France.
[2] The princess's ceremonial room illustrates the pomp and luxury of the 18th century.

[3] and [5] The orange garden and main courtyard of the Hôtel de Sully at no. 62, Rue Saint-Antoine. This splendid example of the Louis XIII style now contains the offices of the national monuments organization.

[4] The imposing Hôtel Lambert, an early work by the architect Louis Le Vau, overlooks the Quai d'Anjou.

[1] and [2] The Hôtel Matignon has served as the official residence of the Prime Minister since 1958.

[Right]
The Hôtel Matignon's main staircase with its multicolored marble endows the building with the pomp and prestige appropriate to a state palace.

[1] The Hôtel de Bourvallais, now used as the Ministry of Justice, stands amid the luxury stores and hotels of Place Vendôme.
[2] The wide doorway of the Hôtel de Lamoignon at no. 24, Rue Pavée in the Marais leads to the Library of the History of Paris.

[3] [4] and [5] Details of doors from l-r: Hôtel de Saint-Aignan, 71, Rue du Temple; Hôtel Lambert, Quai d'Anjou; Medusa's head, Hôtel Amelot de Bisseuil, 47, Rue Vieille-du-Temple.

[6] Doorway to the Hôtel de Chalons Luxembourg, 26, Rue Geoffroy-L'Asnier.
[7] Doorway to the Hôtel Amelot de Bisseuil (or des Ambassadeurs de Hollande), 47 Rue Vieille-du-Temple.

Paris has provided inspiration for countless intellectuals and creative artists over the course of the centuries; Robert de Sorbon's college (later to become the Sorbonne) was already a rival for the universities of Oxford and Bologna as early as the 13th century.

The National Library maintains the royal tradition of book collecting. The introduction of the legal deposit of books in 1537 ushered in a new phase in the capital's cultural development, which was further enhanced by the creation of the *Encyclopedia* in the Age of the Enlightenment. Meanwhile, men began to gather together to enjoy a new drink: coffee. New meeting places sprang up all over Paris, further stimulating the exchange of ideas. The *Procope* played host to La Fontaine, Voltaire, Diderot, D'Alembert, and Verlaine, and even today the *Café de la Paix* is still haunted by the spirits of Maupassant and Zola. Much later the winds of Existentialism would blow literati, politicians, and artists through the doors of the *Café de Flore* and the *Deux Magots*, while the pioneers of style and fashion were drawn to the *Coupole* and the *Dôme*. Montparnasse became the capital of Cubism in the early 20th century; artists from all over the world flocked here to exchange dreams and revel in the tumultuous partying. Night owls would cross paths in the brasseries *Julien* and *Bofinger* or share sophisticated meals in the *Tour d'Argent*.

The spectacle on the streets was paralleled by intense creativity in the theaters. The Folies-Bergère and the Moulin Rouge set pulses racing, while the Comédie Française paid homage to Molière. Paris has never

Arts and Letters

ceased to send creative shock waves across Europe, and the effects can still be felt today. Visitors need only enter the Salé Museum to plunge into Picasso's Parisian Blue Period, or step through the doors of the Musée d'Orsay to become immersed in Caillebotte's scenes of Parisian life.

[1] The Lycée Henri-IV, at the foot of the Clovis Tower, has been a seat of learning since 1791. It was originally called the Lycée Corneille.

[2] The Sorbonne's observatory on Rue Saint-Jacques is equipped with a 6 in. (153 mm) telescope.

The Hôtel de Fleury, the historic site of the École Nationale des Ponts et Chaussées (National School of Bridges and Highways), located at no. 28, Rue des Saints-Pères, boasts an obelisk in the courtyard and a superb staircase inside.

[1] and [2] The Polytechnic School, founded in 1794, is one of France's most famous engineering schools. The bas-reliefs on its façade illustrate its mission to train civil engineers.

[3] The entrance to the School of Medicine, which became the René Descartes University in 2004.

74

[4] The Law Faculty in the Place du Panthéon was built by Jacques-Germain Soufflot.
[5] The Municipal School of Physics and Chemistry in Place Alfred-Kastler, where Pierre and Marie Curie discovered radium.

[2] and [3] The Pharmacy Faculty on the Avenue de l'Observatoire teaches prestigious courses in a historical setting.

[1] Pediment of the large amphitheater in the School of Medicine.

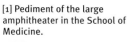

[4] and [6] The Bonaparte Courtyard in the School of Fine Arts echoes elements from architectural landmarks, such as the entrance to the Château d'Anet. [5] The brilliant minds of the Collège de France, founded in 1530 by François I, now pass on their knowledge to students from all social backgrounds.

The Institute of Art and Archeology, or the Michelet Center, was created between 1925 and 1929 by the architect Paul Bigot. This listed monument offers the art history and archeology courses of the Paris-I and Paris-IV universities.

The Palais de l'Institut provides the headquarters for five academies, including the Académie Française, founded in 1635 by Richelieu. The building was designed by Louis Le Vau at the instigation of Cardinal Mazarin. It also contains the Mazarine Library, which preserves some exceptional works among its treasures.

[Following pages] The appropriately named Pont des Arts, situated in the midst of all this culture and learning, links the Institut and the Louvre.

79

[1] The pediments decorating the wings in the Louvre's courtyard were built by the architect Pierre Lescot in 1546.
[2] The pyramid designed by Ieoh Ming Pei was added to the Cour Napoléon in 1989.
[3] Lescot's plans envisaged a square courtyard, now known as the Cour Carré.

[Right] Visitors to the Caryatids' Room are greeted by the Three Graces.

[1] The Caryatids (set in their eponymous room) were sculpted in 1548 by Jean Goujon.
[2] The door opening onto the Quai des Tuileries is called the Lions' Door.
[3] The Tanis Sphinx welcomes visitors to the Egyptian Antiquities section.

[4] The statue of Louis XIV on horseback in the Cour Napoléon was molded from a model created by Bernini.
[5] Napoleon III opted for a more ostentatious style in the reconstruction of the Flora Pavilion and the State Hall.
[6] The Pont des Arts leads straight to the Cour Carré.

[1] The Carnavalet Museum is devoted to the history of Paris, from its origins to the present day. The buildings around the gardens date from the 19th century.
[2] The decoration in the main courtyard came from the workshops of Jean Goujon. The statue of Louis XIV was sculpted by Antoine Coysevox.

The clocks in the Musée d'Orsay are a reminder that the building was a railroad station before it became a depository for the great masterpieces of Impressionism.

[1] Since 1986 the central nave of the old Orsay station has played host to sculpture dating from 1840 to 1875.

[2] This sculptural tribute to Paul Cézanne by Aristide Maillol depicts a woman holding an olive twig.

[3] This sculpture by Emmanuel Frémiet shows Saint Michael slaying the dragon.

4 **5**

6

[4] The imposing rhinoceros in the Musée d'Orsay's forecourt is a bronze sculpture by Alfred Jacquemart. It was unveiled at the 1878 Universal Exhibition.
[5] and [6] The area devoted to French sculpture includes a marble piece from 1868 by Ernest-Eugène Hiolle and bronzes from 1864 by Alexandre Falguière.

[1] The façade overlooking the courtyard of the Hôtel Salé provides a perfect setting for the Picasso Museum.

[2] The Guimet Museum is devoted to Asian art. Its architecture echoes the forms of the Economic and Social Council building by Auguste Perret on the other side of the Place d'Iéna.

[Right] The delights of art and nature in the garden of the Rodin Museum, set in the Hôtel Biron, on the Rue de Varenne.

The Tokyo Palace, a showcase for modern art, displays many features typical of architecture from the 1930s. The terrace overlooking the Seine boasts striking bas-reliefs by Alfred Janniot and a statue by Antoine Bourdelle representing France.

"The Palace of the Museums of Modern Art" was built for the 1937 Universal Exhibition. It now houses the National Museum of Modern Art and the Center of Contemporary Creation.

[1] and [4] The *Flore* and the *Deux Magots*, two historic institutions in Saint-Germain.

[2] The *Closerie des Lilas* was the café that best defined the spirit of Montparnasse.

[3] The *Brasserie Lipp* opened its doors in 1880. This temple of Parisian social life is classified as a historic monument on account of its turn-of-the-twentieth-century decor.

[5] The motto of the *Tour d'Argent*, one of Europe's oldest restaurants, has always been: "There is nothing more serious than pleasure."

[6] The Napoleonic decor and sophisticated food of the *Ledoyen* restaurant have made it a culinary institution for over two centuries.

The *Coupole* was founded in 1927 on the site of an old coal store. This emblem of Montparnasse's Golden Age has witnessed some of the 20th century's high points in art and culture.

The café's sixteen pillars and seventeen pilasters are adorned with thirty-three paintings.

The *Bofinger* brasserie evokes the spirit of Alsace. It has observed the comings and goings on the Place de la Bastille since 1864.

The glass dome designed by Neret and Royer has allowed light into the dining room since 1919.

[1] The *Julien* brasserie preserves the elegance of Parisian Art Nouveau. The red velvet drape opens onto a world that exalts the female figure.

[2] and [3] The sumptuous decor in the dining room is the work of Camille Alphonse Trézel, the master glass painter of this period. His women with floral motifs, a paean to grace and femininity, were inspired by Mucha.

[4] Barbarin, the brasserie's founder, named it after his son Julien.
[5] Segaud was responsible for painting the two peacocks, symbols of paradise and eternity.
[6] Every inch of the sensuous, colorful decor conveys the exquisite tastefulness of Art Nouveau.

[1] The gilt proscenium arch of the Opéra Comique provides a frame for brilliant performances that still attract loyal audiences.
[2] The paintings by Albert Maignan in the main foyer evoke famous comic operas, such as *Les Noces de Jeannette*, *Le Chalet*, and *La Dame Blanche*.

[Right] The caryatids designed by Jules-Félix Coutan support the lower circles in the dazzling auditorium.

POESIE LYRIQUE

[1] The Opéra Garnier, a showcase for dance, brings the Avenue de l'Opéra to a majestic halt. The rooftop crowned with allegorical figures can be seen from far and wide.

[2] When it was unveiled on the main façade, *La Danse* by Jean-Baptiste Carpeaux caused a huge scandal because of the unbridled sensuality of its figures. The original was replaced in 1964 by a copy made by Paul Belmondo.

The Opéra Garnier is one of the finest architectural achievements of the Second Empire. The architect Charles Garnier came up with an opulent, monumental façade that dominates the huge square. This new style (known as Napoleon III) set the tone for bourgeois ornamentation in the late 19th century.

FOLIES BERGERE

FOLIES BERGERE

[1] The façade of the Folies-Bergère is graced by the figure of an uninhibited dancer. Josephine Baker and Mistinguett were among the stars that performed here.
[2] The Art Deco outlines of the Rex have loomed over the great boulevards since 1932.
[3] The Lido on the Champs-Élysées presents extravaganzas of feathers and sequins that are extremely popular with foreign tourists.

[4] The Moulin Rouge, which opened in 1889, symbolizes low-brow Paris, Toulouse-Lautrec, and the cancan.
[5] The Olympia is a legendary concert hall that saw the glory days of the French *chanson*.

[1] The Théâtre de l'Europe, on Place de l'Odéon.
[2] The Théâtre de l'Atelier, on Place Charles Dullin.
[3] The Déjazet, formerly the Théâtre Libertaire Parisien, on the Boulevard du Temple.
[4] The Théâtre Hébertot, at no. 78 bis, Boulevard des Batignolles.

[5] Under the direction of the Bouglione family, the Cirque d'Hiver at 110 Rue Amelot has been exciting children for more than 150 years.

[6] and [7] The Théâtre des Champs-Élysées on Avenue Montaigne, built by Auguste Perret, was decorated with bas-reliefs by Bourdelle and paintings by Maurice Denis.
[8] The Théâtre du Ranelagh and its superb wood-trimmed auditorium at no. 5, Rue des Vignes.
[9] The Théâtre de la Renaissance at no. 20, Boulevard Saint-Martin, owes its existence to an initiative by Dumas and Hugo. It specializes in comedy shows.

Two decorative fountains
embellish the obelisk in the
Place de la Concorde. One
pays tribute to the sea, the
other to rivers.

Paris was confined by walls from the Middle Ages until the 19th century, although additional fortifications gradually pushed back the boundaries a little further.

Although Louis XIV turned Paris into an extravagant city run through with long promenades, the first king who really applied urban planning measures was Henri IV, who set about transforming the far end of the Île de la Cité by creating the Place Dauphine.

The harmony of this square paved the way for the city's five royal squares, including the most elegant and ordered of all, the Place des Vosges. Over the course of the centuries, kings took great pride in their squares and often immortalized themselves by commissioning statues there. The perfect circle of the Place des Victoires is dominated by a statue of the Sun King, as is the Place Vendôme (which was constructed in the same period). The Place de la Concorde was once the Place Louis XV, before becoming the Place de la Révolution and providing the stage for the executions of Louis XVI and Marie Antoinette.

In the same spirit, Napoleon III set in motion major public works, and between 1853 and 1870 Baron Haussmann, the *préfet* of the Seine, widened the axes laid down by Louis XIV and turned them into

Squares and Avenues

imposing boulevards. Haussmann's legacy lives on today in the audacious, visionary city of Paris, caught between a desire for urban planning and a delight in the old town.

[1] The Place Dauphine, named in honor of the future King Louis XIII in the 17th century, was the second royal square, after the Place des Vosges.

[2] The Place des Vosges, the oldest in Paris, is square in shape and is bounded by terraced houses of brick and stone.

[3] and [4] Both Parisians and tourists enjoy strolling through the shady terraces under the square's arcades.

4 5

6

[5] The Queen's Pavilion and the King's Pavilion face each other on opposite sides of the square.
[6] Four fountains adorn the corners of the square, which is dominated by a statue of Louis XIII on horseback.

113

[1] The circular Place des Victoires was built to commemorate the victories of Louis XIV. The statue showing him on horseback was inserted in 1828 to replace an earlier one of him standing.
[2] Detail of the column dedicated to the glory of Napoleon in the Place Vendôme.
[3] Sports cars, luxury hotels, and up-market jewelers set the tone in the Place Vendôme.

[4] During the Reign of Terror a guillotine was set up in the Place de la Concorde and used for numerous executions. It now houses the Hôtel de la Marine, the headquarters of the French Navy, and the Hôtel de Crillon, one of the biggest hotels in the city.

[5] The Obelisk in the center of the square is 33 centuries old and came from the temple of Rameses II in Luxor. It is 75 ft. (23 m) high and its pink granite is completely covered in hieroglyphics.

[1] The rostral columns in the Place de la Concorde were designed by Jacques Hittorff in 1839.
[2] *The Numidian Horses*, sculpted by Guillaume Coustou, were set at the entrance of the Champs-Élysées to replace *The Horses of Marly*.

[3] and [5] Two columns were installed by Claude-Nicolas Ledoux on the Place de la Nation to frame his tollhouses. [4] This monumental ensemble by Aimé-Jules Dalou, *The Triumph of the Republic*, was installed in 1889 to commemorate the centenary of the Revolution.

[1] *The Spirit of the Bastille* overlooks the square from the top of the July Column, built between 1833 and 1840 to commemorate the overthrow of Charles X.
[2] The Rue du Faubourg-Saint-Antoine links Nation with Bastille.
[3] The outlines of the old Bastille prison can be seen on the paving.

The statue in the center of the Place de la République was the work of the Morice brothers (1869), while Aimé-Jules Dalou was responsible for the bas-reliefs illustrating the important events of the Republic.

[1] The tower of the Big Screen building, designed by the Japanese architect Kenzo Tange, looms over the Place d'Italie.

[2] Saint Martin's Gate stands on the site of a gate in Charles V's perimeter wall. It was commissioned by Louis XIV in 1674 to celebrate his victories on the Rhine.
[3] The 13th arrondissement was one of the first neighborhoods in Paris to boast residential tower blocks.

[4] The Rue de Rivoli takes pride of place among Haussmann's boulevards. It links the Place de la Concorde with the Rue Saint-Antoine to form the city's major east-west axis.
[5] Palmier's fountain adorns the Place du Châtelet, on which are situated the Theâtre de la Ville and the Theâtre du Châtelet.

[1] Intersection of Boulevard Montparnasse with Boulevard Raspail.
[2] In the center of the Place Denfert-Rochereau (formerly d'Enfer), the *Lion of Belfort* pays homage to the resistance of Colonel Denfert-Rochereau, the governor of Belfort.
[3] The Enfer tollhouse, built by Claude-Nicolas Ledoux.

[4] At the end of every year, the Avenue of the Champs-Élysées is festooned with decorative lighting.

[5] "The most beautiful avenue in the world", 2,080 yards (1,900 m) long, is dotted with countless luxury stores and theaters that are popular with locals and tourists alike.

[1] and [3] On November 11 every year the State pays tribute at the tomb of the Unknown Soldier, symbolized by the flame that has burned underneath the Arc de Triomphe since 1923.
[2] François Rude's Marseillaise, completed in 1792, represents liberty and the homeland.

[Right] The former Place de l'Étoile became the Place Charles-de-Gaulle on November 13, 1970.

The Eiffel Tower, eternal
symbol of Paris, seen here
with the Trocadéro and the
Champ-de-Mars.

Paris in the 1900s: A Renaissance

The beginning of the 20th century found Parisians gazing through the bright glass roofs of the Grand Palais and the Petit Palais. They turned their back on the upheavals of the previous century and marveled at the modernity taking hold throughout the city.

Paris embraced both progress and frivolity, as exemplified by the Métro entrances decorated by Hector Guimard, the automobile, the telephone, and the cinematograph. Art and technology, exalted by the Universal Exhibitions, became the twin motors of a Belle Époque determined to have a good time. In an effervescent atmosphere that encouraged the mixing of genres, feather boas, top hats, and frills held sway in the Olympia, the city's foremost music hall, and in the cabarets of Montmartre, while nights of revelry could be rounded off in the famed restaurant *Maxim's*.

The Pont Alexandre-III glittered as it crossed the Seine, which was constantly acquiring new buildings along its banks, while the recently opened train stations allowed visitors from the rest of Europe to admire what has become the perennial symbol of France, the Eiffel Tower.

Defying all the technological laws, Gustave Eiffel went beyond accepted limits to build this tower "over a thousand feet tall." The metal structure, then in fact 984 ft. (300 m) high, was initially criticized by famous writers like Maupassant and Verlaine but eventually won acclaim. Its metallic mesh even became a symbol of resistance for Apollinaire and an object of fascination for the Surrealists.

This charismatic construction provided the triumphal doorway to the Universal Exhibition of 1889 and still stands as an emblem for the capital. Paris in 1900 was characterized by modernity, extravagance, and elegance, and its legacy can still be appreciated in today's city.

Gustave Eiffel revolutionized construction by assembling 7,300 tons of girders and rivets in record time. The first floor is situated 187 ft. (57 m) above street level, the second is 377 ft. (115 m) high, and the third (which provides the base for the spire) 902 ft. (275 m).

[1] The extraordinary Eiffel Tower, situated alongside the Seine at the end of the Champs-de-Mars, is an emblem of Paris.
[2] Antoine Bourdelle's bust of Gustave Eiffel, set at the foot of his tower, pays tribute to this visionary.

[1] The Passy Viaduct carrying line 6 of the Métro echoes the metal structure of the nearby tower.

[2] The names of seven-two personalities from the scientific world of the 18th and 19th centuries are inscribed on the first floor.

[3] The television antenna has added an extra 82 ft. (25 m) to the tower's height.

[4] Ever since the dawning of the new millennium, the tower has been lit up every half-hour during the night.
[5] Claire Heller's *Wall for Peace*, at the end of the Champ-de-Mars, celebrates the brotherhood of peoples in front of the Military School.

[Following pages] The Place du Trocadéro-et-du-11-Novembre provides a panoramic view of the Théâtre de Chaillot, the statue of Foch, and the Eiffel Tower.

131

[1] The gardens in the Trocadéro are lined by the statues that Léon Ernest Drivier produced for the 1937 Universal Exhibition.
[2] Paul Valéry's inscription on the pediment of the Palais de Chaillot.
[3] The name of the Court of the Rights of Man was conferred by President François Mitterrand in 1985.

DANS · CES · MURS · VOUÉS · AUX · MERVEILLES
J'ACCUEILLE · ET · GARDE · LES · OUVRAGES
DE · LA · MAIN · PRODIGIEUSE · DE · L'ARTISTE
ÉGALE · ET · RIVALE · DE · SA · PENSÉE
L'UNE · N'EST · RIEN · SANS · L'AUTRE

The Warsaw Fountain and the pools in the Trocadéro Gardens form a popular oasis in hot weather.

[1] The recently renovated glass roof of the Grand Palais creates an imposing presence behind the Pont des Invalides.
[2] The main façade of the Grand Palais and its famous colonnade designed by Henri Deglane.
[3] Georges Récipon's chariots adorn the two entrances to the Grand Palais.

[4] and [5] The Petit Palais contains the City of Paris's superb collections of 19th century paintings and other artworks.

[1] The Austerlitz Station, which began operating in 1834, was the terminus for the Paris-Orléans line. [2] and [3] Saint-Lazare Station, built in 1837, is complemented by Jean-Marie Charpentier's shelter.

[4] The Gare du Nord, which opened in 1864, is the busiest railroad station in Europe and the third busiest in the world for passenger services.

[5] The Gare de Lyon, with its belfry known as the Tour de l'Horloge (Clock Tower), serves the TGV high-speed train network to south-east France.

1

2

[1] The farm produce and coats of arms of thirty-two cities in eastern France embellish the arcade by the entrance to the Gare de l'Est.

[2] The original building, dating from 1850, forms the left-hand section, while the other half, constructed in 1930, is a symmetrical reproduction.

[Right] The decoration on the clock depicts the Rivers Marne and Meuse. The Seine and Rhine are represented on the other side.

[1] The Morris columns are emblems of turn-of-the-twentieth-century Paris but they have recently been subjected to a controversial modernization program.
[2] The cast-iron fountains designed by Richard Wallace are held aloft by the Four Graces (Simplicity, Goodness, Sobriety, and Charity).
[3] The city's coat of arms, dating from the 13th century, is emblazoned on Paris's public street furniture.

Hector Guimard created over 140 entrances to Métro stations between 1900 and 1912. Only eighty-three remain today.

[1] Hector Guimard's masterpiece, the *Castel Béranger* on Rue La-Fontaine, embodies the Art-Nouveau aesthetic of an artist who involved himself in every phase of a building's creation, from the construction work to the interior finishings.

[4] and [5] The doorway to the Maison de Lalique, at no. 40, Cour Albert-1er, is decorated with branches that creep along the wall.
[6] The house at 25 bis, Rue Benjamin-Franklin, built in 1904 by the Perret brothers, left its structure exposed to view. It anticipated the revolution of construction in concrete.

145

[1] The building called Les Chardons (The Thistles) was created in 1903 by Charles Klein. Its structure was made of reinforced concrete, then a new material—although it was employed here with consummate skill.
[2] A beautiful wrought-iron grille adorned with plant motifs opens onto the entrance hall.

[Right] The façade is completely covered with yellow-ocher and almond-green tiles made by Eugène Müller. These are complemented by an original ensemble of thistles and leaves.

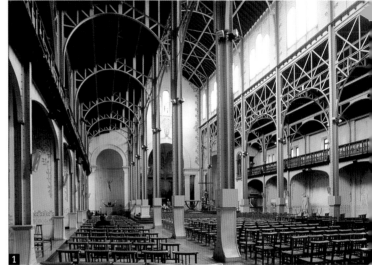

[1] The Church of Notre-Dame-du-Travail on Rue Vercingétorix is unusual because of its structure, made entirely of metal.

[2] The Rue des Immeubles-Industriels (1873) contains workshops and accommodation.

[3] Guimard manifested his love for his wife by building this mansion at no. 122, Avenue Mozart. Here he adapted his work to classical precepts (1909).

[4] The Céramic Hôtel at no. 34, Avenue de Wagram features the combined talents of Jules Lavirotte and the ceramist Alexandre Bigot.

[5] Art Nouveau in a commercial context: the Félix Potin store built by the architect Paul Auscher on the Rue de Rennes.
[6] In 1905 Lavirotte won the prize for the best façade in Paris for his doorway at no. 29, Avenue Rapp.

149

[1] and [2]
Maxim's restaurant, the quintessence of Parisian elegance.

[3] [4] and [5] The dining room in *Maxim's* was decorated by Louis Marnez in 1900. Customers come here not only to eat but also to be seen.

Pierre Cardin's Art Nouveau collection, on display since 2004, brings together furniture and shimmering pottery...

...as well as other *objets d'arts*. They have found an ideal home on the upper floor of *Maxim's*, at no. 3, Rue Royale.

153

Riverside Paris

Paris looks best reflected in the waters of the Seine— particularly at sunset, when the dipping sun gleams on the Right Bank, the Pont-Neuf, and the Île de la Cité, as the river flows lazily by.

The Seine has always been considered the backbone of Paris, from the days of the tribe of the Parisii (a name meaning "boat on the water" in the Celtic Gallic language) to the Romans, who christened Paris Lutetia (meaning "mud"). Hardly a surprise that the city's motto is *Fluctuat nec mergitur* ("Tossed by the waves but never sunk").

The 9-mile (14-km) stretch of the Seine in Paris has always been a busy waterway, bringing the city prosperity and elevating international reputation. These days the wash houses, fishing boats, and vessels laden with wood and wheat been replaced by pleasure boats.

Barges, cruisers, and launches embark from the Pont d'Iéna, the Pont de l'Alma, and the tip of the Île de la Cité carrying thousands of visitors every year. The river affords unbeatable views of the Concorde, the Louvre, the Musée d'Orsay, the green bookstalls, and the colorful parasols on the city's summer beach.

The paths along the banks of the Seine attract walkers, skaters, and cyclists, all eager to appreciate the glorious cradle of the city. There is a constant harmony—in both the bluish tinge of the early morning

And the Seine Runs Right Through the Center

and the romantic glow at dusk—between the Seine and the monuments and citizens of the city, reflecting an equally exquisite balance between sky, water, stone, and spirit.

[1] The launches of the Ministry of Finance allow hard-pressed politicians to travel comfortably between Concorde and Bercy.
[2] Vintage barges anchored to the Quai de Grenelle.
[3] Even today merchandise is transported on the Seine by barge.

4

[4] The tourist boats are generally known as "Bateaux Mouches," though this term is now a registered trademark.

[5] All the romanticism of life on board a barge, right next to the Concorde!

5

[1] A cruise boat passing under the Pont des Arts.
[2] and [3] Barges anchored close to the Eiffel Tower.

[4] and [5] A group of barges are docked together by the Institut, while another one heads off into the sunset.
[6] The Quai de Conti, the headquarters of the river's fire service.

[Following pages]
A barge at anchor in the tranquility of the Pont Neuf.

161

[1] The Allée des Cygnes, an embankment along the river created in the early 19th century. [2] A jogger underneath the Quai d'Anjou.

[3] and [4] The Square du Vert-Galant offers unrivalled views of the Louvre, the Pont-Neuf, and the Pont des Arts.
[5] Companionship on the riverbank.

The bookstalls on the wharfs of the Seine are one aspect of literary Paris that is particularly prized by foreign visitors.

The banks of the Seine in August: The popular Paris Plage (beach) sometimes resembles the beaches in the South of France.

Although the Pont Mirabeau moved Apollinaire to tears, it's functionality isn't so romantic. The bridges of Paris are primarily a means of union and exchange that have permitted the traffic of people and vehicles through the years.

The city's thirty-six bridges, viaducts, and walkways are situated one after another in a steady rhythm along the riverbanks, although one third are concentrated around the Seine's islands.

Nothing remains of the medieval bridges that connected the Île de la Cité to the two banks; these precarious structures incorporating shops and houses were often destroyed and then rebuilt. It was not until the 16th century that Parisians experienced a bridge lined with sidewalks rather than buildings: the Pont Neuf. Its name (the New Bridge) now seems paradoxical, because it is in fact the oldest bridge in Paris.

Completed in 1606 during the reign of Henri IV, it offered a solution to the increasingly pressing problem of communication between the two banks. The Pont Neuf is also one of the most beautiful bridges in Paris, thanks to its statue of Henri IV on horseback and its twelve stone arches. It is complemented by two 17th-century structures: the Pont Marie and the Pont Royal.

Bridge construction intensified in the 19th century, spurring economic and social development. Everything—history, people, cars, the arts, courting couples—converged on these bridges, from the Pont du Carrousel to the Pont de Solférino, from the Pont

From Bridge to Bridge

Louis-Philippe to the Pont Alexandre-III, from the Pont de l'Alma (complete with its famous Zouave statue) to the Pont de Grenelle. The Pont des Arts, a wrought-iron walkway linking the Institut de France with the Louvre, attracts painters and photographers entranced by the view, as well as lovers reveling in its romanticism.

[1] The Pont Charles-de-Gaulle (1996) links the Gare de Lyon with the Gare d'Austerlitz.
[2] Saint Genevieve watches over Paris from the top of a column on the Pont de la Tournelle (1928).
[3] The Pont Louis-Philippe (1833) stretches between Notre-Dame and the Marais, straddling the Île de la Cité.

[4]

[5]

[4] The Pont Marie (1635) is one of the city's oldest bridges. It was once burdened with houses, but these were prohibited in 1769.

[5] The Pont de Bercy acquired another story in 1904 to accommodate line 6 of the Métro.

[1] The Pont d'Austerlitz, (1903), is an arched railroad bridge with a suspended deck now used by Métro line 5.
[2] The Pont Sully (1876), comprises two distinct bridges separated by the tip of the Île de la Cité.
[3] The Pont d'Arcole was the first Parisian bridge made of wrought iron rather than cast iron.

[4]

[4] The Pont de l'Archevêché (1828), a mere 36 ft. (11 m) wide, is one of the city's narrowest bridges.
[5] Taking its name from the double toll charged in the 17th century, the Pont au Double links the Left Bank with Notre-Dame.

[5]

[1] The Pont Neuf and La Samaritaine, a building that once housed a famous department store of the same name.
[2] Loving couples traditionally engrave their names in the Pont Neuf.
[3] Henri IV opened the Pont-Neuf in 1607 but the statue depicting him on horseback was added in 1818, by order of Louis XVIII.

[4] Three hundred-eight five masks sculpted by Germain Pilon are set under the bridge's cornices.
[5] Victor Baltard added ornate columns decorated with the heads of river divinities (1854).
[6] The Pont Neuf was the first stone bridge with sidewalks and no houses.

The Pont Neuf emerged from a major restoration program in 2007 with a new sparkle to its lamp-posts, masks, and Henri IV statue.

The Pont des Arts (strictly speaking the Passerelle—or walkway—des Arts) links the Louvre's Cour Carrée with the Institut.

The original bridge was replaced in 1981 by a replica that preserved its essential characteristics—although its original nine arches have been substituted with seven, in order to align it with the Pont Neuf.

The Pont de la Concorde, stretching between the Quai d'Orsay and the Quai des Tuileries, was built partly with stone salvaged from the demolished Bastille.

[1] The first stone of the Pont Alexandre-III was laid in 1896 in the presence of Tsar Nicholas II and the French president Félix Faure. Its opening coincided with the Universal Exhibition of 1900.
[2] and [3] Major sculptors of the day contributed to the decoration on the bridge.

The tops of the arches of the Pont Alexandre-III are decorated with two compositions by Georges Récipon depicting, top, the Nymphs of the Seine bearing the arms of Paris and, bottom, the Nymphs of the Neva bearing the arms of Russia.

1 **2**

3

[1] The four monumental lampposts were made by the sculptor Henri Gauquié.
[2] Four statues represent the "Four Fames": the Arts, War, Agriculture, and Combat.
[3] Four superb groups of water spirits, complete with fish and shells, stand at the foot of the pillars.

[Following pages] The Pont des Invalides, built in 1854, is the lowest bridge in Paris.

[1] The Zouave on the Pont de l'Alma has experienced flooding.
[2] The Pont des Invalides is decorated with two allegorical groups representing Victory on Land and Victory at Sea.
[3] The imperial eagles adorn the piles of the Pont d'Iéna (1814).

[4] The Debilly walkway was intended as a temporary construction for the Universal Exhibition of 1900. It is now classified as a historic monument.
[5] The Solférino walkway was renamed in 2006 to mark the centenary of the birth of the Senegalese writer and politician Léopold Sédar Senghor.

[1] The Pont de Bir-Hakeim and *France Reborn*, sculpted by Holger Wederkinch.

[2] The Pont Rouelle is a railroad bridge used by the RER's C line.

190

[3] [4] and [5] Gustave Michel's sculptures on the Pont de Bir-Hakeim include depictions of boatmen and blacksmith-riveters, directly integrated into the metal structure.

[1] and [2] Four colossal bronze figures by the sculptor Jean-Antoine Injalbert adorn the stone foundations of the Pont Mirabeau. They represent sea goddesses.

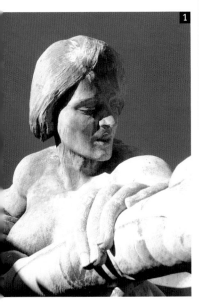

[3]

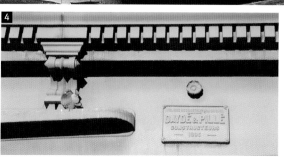

[4]

[3] "Under the Pont Mirabeau runs the Seine": this bridge was thus immortalized by Guillaume Apollinaire in 1913, in an eponymous poem in his collection *Alcools*.

[4] A commemorative plaque commemorates the work of the bridge's builders, Daydé and Pillet.

The Canal Saint-Martin, which opened in 1825, stretches for 3 miles (4.5 km) from the Bassin de la Villette to the Port de l'Arsenal. Its construction was funded by a tax imposed on wine.

The Canal de l'Ourcq, the Canal Saint-Martin, and the Bassin de la Villette form the city's network of canals. These days their banks are imbued with a romantic atmosphere that entices lovers and families to go for leisurely strolls. The Canal Saint-Martin still retains the character of the era in which it was created.

The working-class neighborhood depicted in Marcel Carné's movie *Hôtel du Nord* still resonates along the footbridges, while the chestnut and plane trees rustle at night as if murmuring Arletty's unforgettable comment, "Atmosphere." This is the word that best sums up the Canal Saint-Martin and the Canal de l'Ourcq.

In the early 19th century, Napoleon built a network of waterways in Paris to supply the city with drinking water and create navigation routes. The Canal de l'Ourcq was dug in 1808 between the Ourcq and the Seine. The Empire's engineers excavated the canal as far as the Rotonde of the Place de Stalingrad; in 1825 the waterway was extended by the addition of the Canal Saint-Martin.

The Industrial Revolution sparked a construction boom along the banks of the canals, supplied by barges loaded with cereals, coal, and building materials. Some of today's warehouses recall those feverish days, but the canals are now largely bounded by residential buildings and operate at a more leisurely pace, as the

The Charm of the Canals

barges laden with merchandise have given way to small pleasure boats and passenger services for tourists. When the barges from the Arsenal or La Villette, with their swing bridges, overpasses, and humpback bridges, wait to pass through the canal locks, Paris takes on a provincial air.

[1] and [2] The banks of the Canal Saint-Martin form a pedestrian axis running through the picturesque scenery of Paris's old suburbs.
[3] Rarely has a movie evoked a place as powerfully as *Hôtel du Nord*— even though it was filmed in a studio in Boulogne!

Parisians are rediscovering the canal, with its nine locks and swing and Venetian bridges made of metal. It is undoubtedly one of the city's most romantic settings.

[1] The quiet promenade opposite the Square Villemin has seen fierce battles in its time.
[2] and [3] Passing through the locks is a leisurely affair for all types of barges.

[4] The Canal Saint-Martin offers all the delights of the changing seasons in the heart of Paris.

[1] The workings of the nine locks on the Canal Saint-Martin are a tourist attraction in their own right.

[2] The decline of the industries on the banks has transformed these working-class suburbs into bohemian neighborhoods.

[Right] Apart from the locks, there are also two swing bridges that regulate the traffic on the Canal Saint-Martin.

[1] and [2] The bascule bridge on the Rue de la Crimée, which spans the Canal de l'Ourcq, was built in 1885. The two warehouses in the background were used to store flour and grain.
[3] The Canal Saint-Denis, a branch of the Canal de l'Ourcq, flows gently through La Villette.

[Right] The Bassin de la Villette is the largest artificial expanse of water in Paris. Its imposing Rotonde, built by Ledoux in 1784, was once used to collect tolls on incoming agricultural produce.

[1] [2] and [4]
The port of
Paris-Arsenal
opens onto the
Seine at the
end of the
Canal Saint-
Martin. It was
created in 1983
in the old
moats of the
Bastille to
accommodate
over 200 pleas-
ure boats.

[3] and [5] The iron footbridge
(1895) that straddles the Bassin
de l'Arsenal has served as
a backdrop for numerous videos
and fashion photo shoots.

T he fountains of Paris, symbols of life and renewal, have dispensed precious water with pomp and splendor since the 19th century, when the opening of the Canal de l'Ourcq increased the supply of available water.

The city's numerous aqueducts and watercourses have made it possible to create beautiful sculptural ensembles that feature spraying water. Paris's predilection for commemorative and decorative monuments has led to numerous ornamental fountains that have little practical use. They are frequently inhabited by tritons, nymphs, fauns, and bacchantes, all benevolent creatures associated with water, nature, and abu dance.

Fountains: The Living Springs of Paris

The oldest fountains have been refurbished, or even been completely dismantled and reassembled, as in the cases of the Fontaine Maubuée—the oldest in Paris, dating from the 13th century—and the Fontaine des Innocents, an elegant 16th-century loggia. The remarkable Fontaine des Quatre Saisons, on Rue de Grenelle, is one of the few 18th-century fountains that were a precursor to the forthcoming opulence. From then on, fountains were often used to celebrate a victory, such as the Fontaine de Palmier on the Place du Châtelet.

On the Place de la Concorde, the horrors of the Revolution were washed away by the Fontaine des Mers to the south and the Fontaine des Fleuves to the north. On Place Saint-Michel, the Archangel Michael stands on a rock ready to slay dragons, while on Place Saint-Sulpice the Fontaine des Évêques (Bishops) honors the great preachers of the Louis XIV era. The fountain on the Square de Louvois, the Fontaine Cuvier at the Jardin des Plantes, and the Fontaine des Quatre Parties du Monde opposite the Luxembourg Gardens are splendid examples of the mysterious, allegorical creatures that characterize the fountains and gardens of Paris.

[1] The Fontaine aux Lions in the Place Félix Éboué was originally installed on the Place du Château-d'Eau (now Place de la République).
[2] The fountain on the Place de la Contrescarpe, surrounded by café terraces.
[3] The Square des Combattants-d'Indochine memorial at the Porte Dorée.

The Fontaine du Châtelet (also known as "du Palmier" or "de la Victoire") is remarkable for its sphinxes emitting jets of water.

The Fontaine des Quatre Parties du Monde, designed by Gabriel Davioud in 1874, extends the Avenue de l'Observatoire. Pierre Legrain's globe, Jean-Baptiste Carpeaux's allegory of the four corners of the world, and Emmanuel Frémiet's horses all combine to powerful effect.

[1] Voltaire thought that the Fontaine des Quatre Saisons, at no. 57, Rue de Grenelle, would have looked better in a square.
[2] The two fountains on the Place André Malraux were commissioned from Gabriel Davioud by Baron Haussmann in 1874.
[3] The wild animals of the Fontaine Cuvier are situated close to the Jardin des Plantes.

Students and tourists congregate around the Fontaine de la Place Maubert (or Place de la Contrescape) and while away the time on the square's café terraces.

[Left] Detail of the Fontaine des Quatre Saisons, sculpted by Edme Bouchardon between 1739 and 1747.

[1] The Fontaine aux Lions de Nubie became too small for the Place de la République; it was enlarged in 1867 and transferred to La Villette.
[2] The Fontaine de la Place Edmond Rostand, set in front of the Panthéon, displays a nymph and a triton.
[3] The Fontaine de Jarente, built in 1783, on the Impasse de la Poissonnerie in the Marais.

215

[1] The Fontaine de Visconti, on Place Saint-Sulpice, is also called the fountain of "the four cardinal points," because of the presence of four statues of bishops: Bossuet, Fénelon, Massillion, and Fléchier.

[2] The fountain on the Square de Louvois, on Rue de Richelieu.

[3] The Fontaine des Haudriettes was installed on Rue des Archives in 1770.

4

5

6

[4] The Fontaine des Innocents, built in 1549 in the heart of Les Halles, commemorates Henri II's triumphant entrance into the city.
[5] A popular market sets up its stalls around the fountain on the Place Monge.
[6] The fountains with spheres designed by Pol Bury (1985) provide a perfect foil for the Palais-Royal.

[1] The Fontaine Molière was built in 1844 by the architect Louis Visconti. It was the first of a non-royal subject to be built from national subscription.

[2] The Fontaine Saint-Michel is dominated by a statue of the dragon-slaying saint. It was commissioned by Haussmann in order to hide an unsightly gabled wall exposed by the demolitions undertaken to make way for the Avenue Saint-Michel.

[3] The Fontaine de la Reine, at the junction of Rues Greneta and Saint-Denis.
[4] The Fontaine de Mars, also known as the Fontaine du Gros Caillou, (1806) forms part of a group of seventeen fountains commissioned by Napoleon.
[5] The Fontaine de la Croix du Trahoir, on Rue de l'Arbre-Sec, is adorned with bas-reliefs (originally they were just paintings) by Jean Goujon.

...with water from safe springs.
[3] For a long time the water emerging from the artesian well in la Butte-aux-Cailles at a temperature of 82°F (28°C) supplied the local swimming pool.

[Right] There are eighty-eight Wallace fountains in Paris providing drinking water from March to November. They are maintained by the Eau de Paris, a firm devoted to supplying citizens with top-quality water.

[1] The Montsouris reservoir contains drinking water destined for southern Paris.
[2] Artesian well on Lamartine Square. After the cholera epidemic of 1832, the city authorities drilled wells to supply Paris...

220

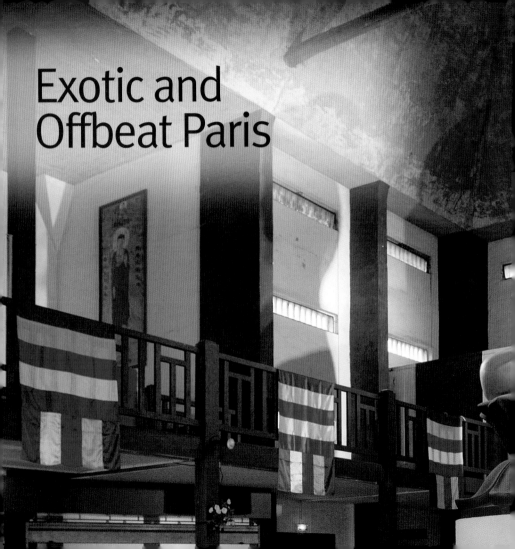

Exotic and Offbeat Paris

A part from its historical, architectural, and artistic heritage, Paris boasts another great asset: its ethnic communities. The city provides exciting journeys to faraway places without ever having to cross frontiers.

Ever since its earliest days Paris has always been a mix of cultures. From sidewalk to sidewalk, from church to church, from restaurant to restaurant, the world is revealed here in all its diversity, with all its particularities, in everyday Parisian life. The sub-Saharan African community that has settled in the neighborhood of Château-Rouge, for example, has created a strikingly distinctive atmosphere with its hairdressers and restaurants.

The balalaikas and violins of the Russians who fled the 1917 Revolution are now found in the vicinity of the Orthodox cathedral on Rue Daru, while some of the *izbas* (Russian wooden houses) left over from the 1867 Exhibition were used as homes after being transplanted to the 16th arrondissement. This neighborhood's special atmosphere is derived not so much from the restaurants advertising their European menus but more from the feeling of breathing the air of another country.

Similarly, you only need to drink a pint of beer in one of the city's wonderful pubs to evoke the inviting allure of Ireland, or enter the Passage Brady to experience a district of Mumbai, or shop in the market in Ménilmontant to catch a snatch of Caribbean music wafting out from behind a fruit stall.

Paris: Showcase of the World

Various communities share Parisian neighborhoods, or sometimes keep an area for themselves, as in the case of the Jewish area on Rue des Rosiers, with its five synagogues and countless falafel joints catering to tourists, or the 13th arrondissement, inextricably linked with the Far Eastern community.

[1] and [2] The former colonial school on the Avenue de l'Observatoire, designed in a neo-Moorish style by Adolphe Yvon, now houses the International Institute of Public Administration. [3] The *Pletzel* ("little place" in Yiddish) on Rue des Rosiers.

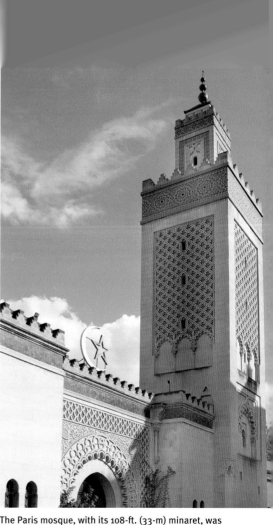

The Paris mosque, with its 108-ft. (33-m) minaret, was built on 2½ acres of land (one hectare) in 1926. It is the biggest mosque in France.

[1] This façade on Place du Caire is decorated with Egyptian-style masks and friezes, a legacy of the craze sparked by Napoleon's expeditions to Egypt.

[2] and [3] The former Museum of the Colonies in the Palace of the Porte Dorée is now the Museum of the History of Immigration.

[4] The Fontaine du Fellah, at the entrance to the Vaneau Métro station, is further evidence of the Napoleonic enthusiasm for all things Egyptian.
[5] and [6] The hammams (Turkish baths) on the Boulevard de la Chapelle offer one of the delights of Oriental culture in the heart of Paris.

[1] and [3] The Saint Alexander Nevsky Cathedral on Rue Daru is dedicated to the Grand Prince of Novgorod, one of Russia's most popular saints.

[4] Four *izbas* were preserved in the Villa Beauséjour after the 1867 Universal Exhibition.

[Right] Ganesh invites you to take a trip to India on the Passage Brady.

[1] and [3] The Passage Brady is dotted with numerous Indian and Pakistani restaurants, specialist grocery stores, bazaars, and hairdressers.
[2] Video rental outlets stock the latest Bollywood movies.

[4] and [6] Most of the city's Far Eastern population is concentrated between the Porte de Choisy and the Porte d'Italie. This area constitutes the Parisian Chinatown.

[5] The Maison Loo, built on the Rue de Courcelles by a rich collector, is a six-story pagoda, now used as an art gallery.

[7] Chinese-style roofs nestle in the shadows of the Olympiade skyscrapers in the 13th arrondissement.

[1] The International Buddhist Institute is set in the Cameroon Pavilion, built for the Colonial Exhibition of 1931. It was turned into a pagoda to be used as a place of worship in 1977.

[2] The Great Pagoda contains a large statue of Buddha, 33 ft. (10 m) high.

[3] The Great Pagoda, with the Wheel of the Law on its façade.

[4] The enormous Buddha was the work of the Yugoslav sculptor François Mozès.

[5] A small traditional Tibetan temple was built in 1985 for the Kagyu Dzong Center. It was designed in accordance with Tibetan precepts.

T

he imposing length of the great boulevards linking the Opéra with the Place de la République offers an exciting range of stores and cafés, theaters and hotels.

This ancient promenade, created by Louis XIV, achieved its finest hour in the first half of the 19th century, when a leisured class enriched by property speculation introduced passages and covered galleries to make their shopping more agreeable. Now they would no longer have to endure bad weather or horses in the streets. These havens of peace, designed for leisurely perusing, gave new meaning to taking a stroll, one that reflected Parisian notions of elegance and leisure.

The passages form a veritable maze of stone, glass, and mosaics. They are sometimes discreetly hidden between two buildings but are often emblazoned with a commemorative plaque. An enterprising spirit can use them to take a smart short cut from the Opéra to the Palais-Royal: from the Galerie Verdeau, along the Passage Jouffroy, then the Passage des Panoramas and, finally, the Galerie Vivienne and the Galerie de Colbert (in its day, considered the most attractive of all these haunts). This labyrinthine journey is freely available to all and offers a host of remarkable sights and surprises.

Although the erstwhile glory of some passages has been preserved—the Galerie Vivienne, for example, with its high, ornate ceilings, its pilasters, and its mosaic by the famous Italian ceramist Faccina—the splendor of others has been recovered through refurbishment, as in the case of the Passage des Panoramas, a favorite of 19th-century *flâneurs*. The colors of these passages are

Secret Courtyards and Passages

endowed with subtle hues by glass roofs, creating a twilight atmosphere in a unique, picturesque environment. Even today, a detour past a caryatid or an intriguing sign can lead to adventure in a passage between two worlds.

[1] and [2] La Cour de l'Étoile d'Or (courtyard of the Golden Star) in Faubourg Saint-Antoine boasts a sundial dating from 1751.

[3] The wisteria on Rue Cuvier, the oldest in Paris.

The Cour de Rohan consists of a series of three small courtyards. It once belonged to a hotel that accommodated the bishops of Rouen (hence the name, albeit corrupted).

At the time of the Industrial Revolution, the houses in the Villa Mulhouse (16th arrondissement) were intended for workers.

[1] The neoclassical houses in the Hameau Boileau were built in 1838 on property owned by Nicolas Boileau.
[2] The Rue du Jardinet (6th arrondissement), which opens onto the Cour de Rohan.
[3] The houses on Rue de la Liberté, to the east of the 19th arrondissement, were confined to a single story because of the instability of the subsoil.

[1] The Passage de la Fonderie, on Rue Jean-Pierre-Timbaud.
[2] A small passage hidden amidst the lush vegetation of the Villa Poissonnière.
[3] The store fronts on the Passage de l'Ancre are notable for their pastel decoration.

[4] The smallest house in Paris, at no. 39 Rue du Château-d'Eau. This curiosity, just over a yard wide, was the result of an inheritance dispute.
[5] This narrow passage leading onto the Rue Raynouard is called the Rue des Eaux.
[6] The Rue des Degrés, just 19 ft. (5.75 m) long, is the shortest in Paris; it is in fact little more than a staircase.

[1] and [5] The Rue Cremieux, a pedestrian-only street lined with small, two-story houses, has a provincial feel.
[2] The small passage behind the carriage entrance on the Rue Oudinot.
[3] The Cour du Commerce-Saint-André displays remains of Philip Augustus's city wall.

[4] The Cour des Fabriques, in the Popincourt
neighborhood, once the domain of metalworkers.

245

The Galerie Vivienne, decorated with nymphs and goddesses, was funded by successful property surveyors. It opened in 1823 as a rival to the neighboring Galerie Colbert.

The Galerie Vivienne, 577-ft. (176-m) long, houses book-shops, restaurants, and art galleries under its superb glass roof. It was classified as a historic monument in 1974.

The Passage du Caire, in the heart of the Sentier, is lined with clothing stores. Its length of 1,214 ft. (370 m) makes it the longest such arcade in Paris.

[1] The tiny Passage Beaujolais links Rue Richelieu to Rue Beaujolais.
[2] The Cour des Trois-Frères in Faubourg Saint-Antoine preserves traces of its furniture-making tradition on its walls.
[3] The Cour de l'Ours is still the location of cabinet-making and upholstery workshops.

[4] The Passage Choiseul, built around
1925, is one of the longest in Paris, at
623 ft. (190 m).
[5] Two rows of buildings stand opposite each other, linked by a glass
canopy.

[1] The Passage des Panoramas links the great boulevards with the Bourse neighborhood.
[2] The Musée Grévin is nestled among the cafés and shops on the Passage Jouffroy. This wax museum, founded in 1882, contains representations of more than 300 famous personalities.

The Passage du Grand-Cerf, built in 1835, stands opposite the more modest Passage du Bourg-l'Abbé.

The Passage Verdeauin in the Grange Batelière neighborhood is a mecca for antiquarian book collectors in search of rare treasures.

The Passage Choiseul, packed with unpretentious stores, has barely changed since its construction in 1829.

Paris is not only inhabited by men and women but also a fabulous range of animals and mythological creatures, captured in the city's decorative details, that speak the language of symbolism.

Visitors need only to take a short walk in order to come upon sculpted pediments on doors and windows, or the ornate masks on door knockers, balconies, and entrances to buildings. A stroll can become a safari, with a veritable menagerie enlivening the streets, houses, and hotels, as in the case of the Hôtel Salé (now the Picasso Museum), where dogs' heads, the heraldic emblem of the Aubert family, decorate the main courtyard. Elsewhere, numerous exotic species from afar bear witness to the colonial era and the inspiration of Orientalism.

The lion is the undisputed king of Parisian façades, but other, sometimes surprising animals emerge from carved stone as well: an elephant embraces a door with its big ears; a peacock splays its tail above a porch, while dragons and snakes dispel intruders. Domesticated animals are here, too: rams' heads are the most common, but cats, dogs, cows, donkeys, and beehives also nod at the rural amidst the urban.

Various professions utilize these symbols to express pride in their trade; for example, a cow would be depicted on the façade of

Fabulous Beasts and Curious Decorations

a butcher's shop, restaurants, and slaughterhouses, just as a fish would also be displayed at a seafood market.

Large horses' heads adorn the railings of the George-Brassens gardens, recalling the Vaugirard horse market and slaughterhouse that once stood on this spot.

[1] The façade of the famous artists' squat at no. 59, Rue de Rivoli has long been smiling down at passers-by...while awaiting development.
[2] Place Frénel in Belleville. The sign warns onlookers to distrust words.
[3] The façade at no. 39, Avenue George-V during its renovation in 2007: urban surrealism!

[4] The façade of the Musée Baccarat on the Place des États-Unis suggests the luxury of the interior.
[5] The *Passe-Muraille*, a tribute to Marcel Aymé, in the heart of Montmartre.

[1] The fish market on Rue Castagnary pays homage to fishermen.
[2] Mile zero for all roads in France, on the forecourt of Notre Dame.

[3] In 1797, the Convention set 16 one-meter strips into marble in various parts of Paris to familiarize the populace with the new measurement. Only four have survived.

[4] The feudal house tax mark of the Coutures Saint-Gervais on the walls of the Hotel Salé.
[5] Tromp-l'oeil on Rue Juliette-Dodu (10th arrondissement).
[6] The Church of Saint-Christophe-de-Javel offers protection for motorists.

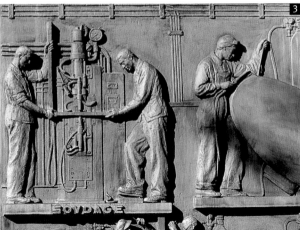

[1] The ships depicted on the barracks on Rue du Faubourg-Poissonnière recall the departure of young recruits to Canada.
[2] A locomotive adorns the pediment of the "Échos de l'exportation" at no. 4, Rue Martel.
[3] Bas-reliefs on the old technical center at no. 87, Rue de Grenelle.
[4] A former soldering institute at no. 32, Boulevard de la Chapelle.

[5] Bas-relief in Porte-Maillot by Aimé-Jules Dalou, dedicated to Émile Levassor, a pioneer of the fuel-powered automobile.
[6] The medical center for railroad workers on the Place de l'Abbé-Georges-Hénocque is adorned with a locomotive.

263

[1] and [3] Dogs decorate the garden courtyard and the service quarters of the Hôtel Salé (3rd arrondissement).
[2] A ferocious wolf is ready to pounce on hapless passers-by on the Rue Oudinet, in the 7th arrondissement.
[4] A dog keeps watch over the Passage des Acacias.

[5] A peacock with its train fully extended at no. 19, Rue Octave-Feuillet (16th arrondissement).
[6] The *Chez Julien* restaurant on Rue du Pont Louis-Philippe is decorated with birds.
[7] A rooster, the emblem of France, stands in front of the National Library on Rue Vivienne.

[1] Dragon at no. 50, Rue de Rennes.
[2] Griffin at no. 4, Rue de Ruysdaël.
[3] Ram's head by the doorway to the Hôtel d'Alméras, at no. 26, Rue des Francs-Bourgeois.

[4] A lion surveys the Canal Saint-Martin from the Rue des Vinaigriers (10th arrondissement).
[5] This steer is a reminder that the Parc Georges-Brassens was once a slaughterhouse (15th arrondissement).

267

A visit to one of the cemeteries
of Paris attracts both locals
and tourists seeking moments
of quiet reflection.

The dark past of Paris is far less seductive than its eye-popping exterior splendor. For evidence of this, consider the Middle Ages, a period that saw the birth of Les Halles, a market know as the city's "stomach"—and its cemetery.

For centuries this huge square served as the last resting place for Parisians, whose corpses piled up in pits, with the consequent danger of epidemics, while traders and their customers conducted business above them. By the 14th century, the bodies laid to rest here were barely contained by the soil, but it wouldn't be until 1780 that this mass grave was closed and then reopened in 1785 when they were moved to an underground bone repository in an old quarry beyond the city gates known as the "Tombe-Issoire". The remains of some 6 million people were crammed inside it. The catacombs of Denfert-Rochereau that visitors can see today are the result of an early 19th-century refurbishment of this site. The

bones have been arranged in astonishingly regular rows of tibias and femurs interspersed with skulls, stretching for hundreds of yards into the distance.

In 1803 the Père-Lachaise Cemetery was established in eastern Paris, and this was soon followed by the Montparnasse cemetery to the south in 1824, and that of Montmartre to the north in 1825. In a maze of tombs and trees, the paved roads and rustic paths of the Père-Lachaise lead to the graves of famous personalities like Molière, La Fontaine, Oscar Wilde, and Jim Morrison.

Cemeteries and Catacombs

In contrast, Montparnasse Cemetery is a flat, well-ordered garden, a haven of peace for Charles Baudelaire, Guy de Maupassant, Jean-Paul Sartre, and Simone de Beauvoir. Funerary art comes into its own in these cemeteries, where monuments and sculptures reach remarkable heights of expression.

In order to deal the overcrowding of the cemeteries, it was decided to transfer the skeletons from their mass grave to the catacombs, former underground quarries dating from the late 18th century. A small section can be visited on the Place Denfert-Rochereau.

1

[1] and [3] Visitors can stroll among the meticulously arranged bones. [2] The inscription over the entrance to the burial chamber reads "Stop! This is the Empire of Death."

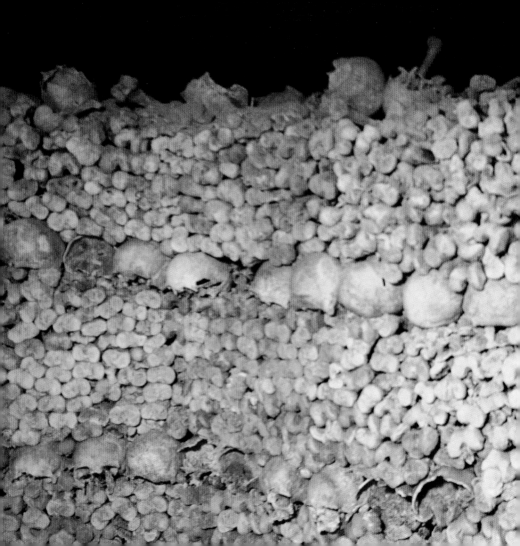

OSSEMENTS·DU
CIMETIERE·DES
INNOCENTS
DÉPOSÉS·LE
2 JUILLET 1809

[Previous pages] The remains from the Cemetery of the Innocents were placed in the catacombs from 1786 to 1809. It is calculated that the bones of some 4 million people rest in this tomb.

[1] The tomb of Lafayette in the Picpus cemetery is situated alongside that of the martyrs of the Revolution.
[2] and [3] The tall Montparnasse Tower dominates the cemetery.

[4] The grounds of the Mill of Charity, built in the early 17th century by the friars of Saint-Jean-de-Dieu, were turned into dancing gardens after the Revolution. When the City of Paris decided in 1824 to use the large space for the Montparnasse cemetery, the mill served as the guardhouse. It now stands empty.

[5] Charles Baudelaire, one of the cemetery's most visited residents.

[1] and [4] 34,000 dead, both famous and anonymous, are buried in the Montparnasse cemetery. [2] Fans leave Métro tickets on Serge Gainsbourg's grave in memory of his famous song "Le poinçonneur des Lilas" ("The Ticket Collector of the Lilas").

[3] Numerous works by some of the 20th century's foremost sculptors can be found on the graves of both celebrities and ordinary citizens.

The cemetery of Père-Lachaise, the biggest in Paris, contains over 70,000 graves, including those of rock stars, distinguished soldiers, and intellectuals, as well as common folk.

[1] The tomb of Cino del Duca, a publisher, patron of the arts, and philanthropist.

[3] After the transfer of the remains of Abelard and Heloise, Molière, and La Fontaine in 1817, the cemetery of Père-Lachaise was enlarged substantially.

[2] The grave of the journalist Victor Noir, renowned for his virility, is curiously well worn on a very particular spot.

[Right] *Grief*, a marble statue on the grave of Marie-Geneviève Gamichon.

[1] Tomb of the Raspail family.
[2] The thoroughfares designed by the architect Théodore Brongniart in 1803 lead to the neoclassical chapel.
[3] All the graves in the Père-Lachaise have an original touch, whether they are occupied by famous people or humble citizens.

MAMETTE
*Quand je ne serai plus
mettez sur moi des violettes
et du mimosa.*

[4] Molière and La Fontaine, two brilliant writers side by side.
[5] The cemetery, a veritable open-air sculpture museum, contains a wealth of statuary in various styles.

Natural Paris

The former hunting grounds of
the Bois de Vincennes were
opened to the public during
the reign of Louis XV.

The Bois de Boulogne and the Bois de Vincennes, the remains of the huge forest that surrounded Lutetia in the 1st century AD, are the city's two green lungs, situated at opposite cardinal points—to the west and east of Paris, respectively. They were revamped under the Second Empire.

Napoleon III, in his drive to make Paris healthier and more beautiful, gave Jean-Charles Alphand the extravagant title Ingénieur en Chef du Service des Promenades (Engineer in Chief of the Promenades Service) and instructed him to landscape the two woods, which had been largely destroyed during the Revolution. The Bois de Boulogne, situated between Boulogne and Neuilly, attracted the elegant inhabitants of western Paris. After opening in 1852, it became the era's most fashionable meeting place, where courting couples could while away entire days. Alphand laid delightful avenues and footpaths leading through newly planted pine and oak groves to two artificial lakes linked by a waterfall. The wood embraces the Parc de Bagatelle, the glasshouses of Auteuil, the restaurant *Le Pré Catelan*, and the Jardin d'Acclimatation, which has been developed over the years.

After lovingly restructuring the Bois de Boulogne as a gift to the city, Napoleon III decided in 1857 to make a similar gesture to eastern Paris, where most of the neighborhoods were working-class. He thus created a similar park in the other part of the original forest opened up by Louis XV. Alphand dreamed up a romantic getaway by constructing four terraced lakes dotted with islands containing restaurants and secret grottos. Like the Bois de Boulogne, it

A Stroll in the Woods

would also boast a hippodrome. In the early 20th century, the Bois de Vincennes, which had constantly undergone transformations, opened its gates to a zoo and the Floral Park—popular with strolling families on Sundays—while the Tibetan Temple of the International Buddhist Institute offers a complete change of scenery.

286

[1] The Pré Catelan is a 20-acre (8-hectare) garden that was created within the Bois de Boulogne in 1954.

[2] [3] and [4] The Kiosque de l'Empereur was built on the Lower Lake by Napoleon III in 1857 for the exclusive use of the Imperial couple.

[Following pages] Rowboats can be rented on the Lower Lake, whether for relaxation or vigorous exercise.

289

[Right] The pavilion on the Île de Reuilly, in the center of Lake Daumesnil.

[1] and [3] The Bois de Vincennes, the green lung of east Paris, is endowed with four expanses of water and several streams flanked by tree-lined footpaths. [2] The Lac Daumesnil, like the Lac des Minimes, offers the chance to rent a rowboat.

During the Second Empire, parks, gardens, and neighborhood squares began to appear all over Paris courtesy of Jean-Charles Alphand, Haussmann's official landscaper.

Napoleon III continued to promote greater health for the people of the city and, following the example of London, also sought to offer the working classes oases of greenery. The Parc des Buttes-Chaumont is the archetypical Haussmann park, with landscaping used to create idealized "natural" scenery. It is embellished by romantic but totally artificial details, like the "Pyrenean" grotto and the Sibylline temple dominating the island. Its steep mounds and interlinked paths make it one of the most charming places in Paris.

To the south, the Parc Montsouris, similarly set on the site of an old quarry, is replete with contrived romanticism. The lake, bordered by weeping willows and with swans swimming across it, is complemented by grottos and a waterfall. In order to hide the railroad tracks that once crossed the park, Alphand dreamed up ravines lined with pine trees.

The undulating lawns, bridges, and tearoom combine to form an English-style garden where students from the nearby University love to come and relax. The Parc Monceau combines different styles of landscaping but Haussmann primarily drew on 18th-century precepts to arrive at its definitive format. Originally the property of the Duke of Chartres, the garden was first planted in 1778, with an emphasis on the picturesque. This folly—a sublime illusion studded with Dutch windmills, Roman temples, feudal ruins, and pyramids—was

Haussmann's Parks

purchased by the City of Paris in 1860 and then redesigned by Alphand.

The garden, with its aristocratic air, benefited from Alphand's last flights of fancy, including the addition of new species of trees that form a perfect complement to the lake.

[1] The Parc des Buttes-Chaumont and its 164-ft. (50-m) high rock, born from a whim of Napoleon III.

[2] and [4] The name of the Suicide Bridge is self-explanatory.

[3] The rock is crowned by a Sibylline temple built by Gabriel Davioud in 1869.

[5] Apart from its unique scenery, the Parc des Buttes-Chaumont also offers a panoramic view of the hill of Montmartre and the Sacré-Coeur.

The Parc Montsouris, commissioned by Napoleon III and Baron Haussmann, is an enormous English-style garden created between 1867 and 1878 by the engineer Jean-Charles Alphand.

Its lake and series of
waterfalls bring a welcome
coolness in summer.

This quiet, shady park boasts over 1,400 different types of trees, most of them over a hundred years old. It is also crossed by the GR1 hiking trail.

The flowerbeds and groves are arranged to fit in with the panoramic views.

[Following pages] The Parc du Champ-de-Mars, very close to the Trocadéro, was land-scaped in the French style, complete with an artificial grotto.

[1] The Parc Monceau, created in the late 18th century by the landscape architect Thomas Blaikie, was enlarged and redesigned by Alphand during the Second Empire to create the illusion of natural harmony. [2] and [3] A pyramid and obelisk inspired by Freemasonry decorate the paths of the Parc Monceau.

[4] The rotunda, a tollhouse designed by Claude Nicolas Ledoux, was added in 1784.
[5] and [6] The trees in the park mostly belong to rare species and the lush vegetation gives visitors the impression that they are in a rural setting.

Miniature boats with patch-
work sails cruising on the pool
in the Jardin du Luxembourg.

Gardens of kings, gardens of queens: some patches of greenery are inextricably linked with the royal history of Paris. Their symbolic resonance has often made them targets but their spirit has survived unscathed.

In 1564 Catherine de Medici built a palace with a sumptuous garden in the Tuileries and turned it into a fashionable rendezvous for parties and firework displays. In 1664 André le Notre, on the orders of the King's chief minister Jean-Baptiste Colbert, redesigned the palace garden around a central avenue lined with French-style flowerbeds, thus opening it up to the west and foreshadowing the Champs-Élysées. The Jardin des Tuileries, embellished by the Arc de Triomphe du Carrousel, the Orangerie Museum, and the Jeu de Paume, never fails to astonish both Parisians and tourists alike.

The Jardin du Luxembourg, in its turn, sets off the palace of Marie de Medici, built in 1617 (it now houses the Senate). Italian elements were added in 1623, when it was provided with water via an ingenious aqueduct to supply its fountain, enormous flowerbeds, and orchards. Despite further transformations in the 19th century, the Jardin du Luxembourg still displays a very "feminine" style.

The more discreet garden of the Palais-Royal is a haven of tranquility that has nevertheless been involved in major episodes of French history. Built by Richelieu in 1630, it was nicknamed the "capital of Paris," such was its importance in the political arena. Nowadays its intrigues have been superseded by the pleasures of strolling in a garden surrounded by arcades, not far from the columns designed by Daniel Buren for the courtyard leading to the Comédie Française.

Historical Gardens

The Jardin des Plantes is the descendant of the royal garden of medicinal plants created in 1626 under Louis XIII. It opened its doors to medical students in 1640 and became a scientific club run by Buffon during the Enlightenment. Its combination of elegance and erudition, as exemplified by its tropical glasshouses and rare species in the French-style flowerbeds, is a reflection of the city from which it sprang.

[1] The numerous statues decorating the paths in the Jardin du Luxembourg make it seem like an open-air museum.
[2] and [3] The Marie de Medici Fountain was built by Salomon de Brosse in the style of Italian grottos, but the sculptures are the work of Auguste Ottin.

[4] The Jardin du Luxembourg lies in the heart of the Latin Quarter, with the Panthéon as a backdrop.
[5] Satyrs and fauns taunt passers-by on the Boulevard Saint-Michel.

[1] and [2] The pools, fountains, and exotic trees make the Jardin du Luxembourg a veritable oasis in the heart of Paris.

[3] Detail of the Medici
Fountain.
[4] Pediment of the
Palais du Luxembourg,
now used as the Senate.
[5] Beekeeping enthusi-
asts gathered around
a hive.

[Following pages]
Although French in style,
the Jardin du
Luxembourg, built by
Salomon de Brosse,
borrows elements from
the Italian Renaissance.

[1] A ferris wheel is set up every year in the Jardin des Tuileries, providing panoramic views of central Paris.

[2] As in the Jardin du Luxembourg, the large pool is taken over by miniature sailboats.

[3] The Arc de Triomphe du Carrousel, built in 1808, served as the gateway to the Tuileries.

Reading by the edge of the pools or lazing around next to the flowerbeds: these are just two of the pastimes on offer in the Jardin des Tuileries, a stone's throw from the Louvre.

The Tuileries are dotted with statues by some of the greatest sculptors of all time. Rodin's *Kiss* is surrounded by works by Maillol and other contemporary artists, forming an open-air gallery.

[1] [3] and [right] Today's Jardin des Plantes, the inheritor of the royal garden of medicinal plants, was opened to the public in 1640. Three glasshouses, two of which are open to the public, preserve plants from all over the world.
[2] Not far from the zoo in the Jardin des Plantes, sculpted animals adorn the footpaths.

In 1780, much to the amusement of his contemporaries, the Duke of Orléans built the arcades and shops lining the Palais-Royal to raise money to pay his huge debts.

In the late 18th century, the gardens of the Palais-Royal became a stage for political debate and, above all, licentiousness.

The urban renewal of 19th-century Paris incorporated social and environmental policies that were instigated, from 1854 onward, by a Promenades and Plantations Service through the creation of numerous green spaces.

Apart from the great gardens drawn up in the Second Empire, new squares began to appear in areas that had previously been built up. The Square Saint-Jacques, followed by the Square des Arts-et-Métiers, became the first in a long series of projects designed to establish new spaces. The Square Montholon and the Square de la Trinité, which opened up new traffic routes, were perfect complements to Haussmann's boulevards, as were monuments like the Square Louvois, set in front of the extension to the National Library.

The squares in front of municipal buildings, such as the Square du Temple in the 4th arrondissement and the Square de Montrouge in the 14th arrondissement, are fine examples of landscaping with lawns available for public use. In some neighborhoods these facilities are truly idyllic—the Square des Batignolles, in particular, is one of the most beautiful to have been created under the Second Empire.

Parisian squares, unlike their English equivalents, were always open to the public. City planners in the 20th century complied with this tradition by endowing deprived outlying neighborhoods with new leisure areas.

The Parc Georges-Brassens occupies the site of the old Vaugirard horse market and

Squares and Gardens

slaughterhouse, as the horses' heads on the railings indicate; the huge Parc André-Citroën occupied the space left by the closure of a Citroën factory. The Parc de Belleville was installed on a hill, at a height of 354 ft. (108 m), to provide a distinctive vantage point overlooking the city.

[1] The Square de Vert-Galant, at the tip of the Île de la Cité.
[2] The Square Recamier, one of the smallest in Paris (7th arrondissement).
[3] The Avenue des Champs-Élysées is bordered by delightful gardens adorned with fountains.

The floral promenade above the arches of the Viaduc des Arts follows the path of an old rail line for 3 mi. (4.7 km).

[1] and [2] The Parc de Bagatelle, with its famous rose garden, is a mixture of untouched natural scenery and well-kept gardens.
[3] The Jardins de l'Arsenal are a haven of tranquility situated right next to the Bastille.

[4] The Square Boucicaut is named after the founder of the Bon Marché department store, which stands just opposite.
[5] The Catherine Labouré vegetable garden is open to the public.

[1] Vines can be seen growing on the hills of Montmartre, in the heart of Paris.

[2] The Parc Georges-Brassens has replaced the Vaugirard horse market and abattoirs, although the clock tower of the old auction hall still stands tall in the center.

[3] The Square de l'Île-de-France contains a memorial to victims of Nazi concentration camps (4th arrondissement).
[4] The Square des Batignolles is modeled on an English garden.
[5] Striking decorations on the Square René-le-Gall (13th arrondissement).

[1] Flowers grow alongside the paths in the Jardin du Ranelagh in the 16th arrondissement.
[2] The Square Violet, a secluded spot in the 15th arrondissement.
[3] The Parc André-Citroën stands on the site of an old automobile factory.

4

5

[4] The Square Vert-Galant ("Green Gallant") bears the nickname bestowed on Henri IV for his relentless womanizing.
[5] The Square René-Le-Gall contains features typical of the 1930s, such as its neoclassical obelisks, its clipped hedges, and its summerhouses shrouded in climbing plants.

The Parc de Bercy was laid on the site of old vineyards that were the center of the world's trade in wine and spirits in the 19th century.

[1] The romantic garden in the Parc de Bercy is dotted with remarkable trees and is designed with a central theme of water.

[2] The orange grove forms part of an ensemble that also includes a rose garden, a kitchen garden and a maze.

Village Paris

This hill dedicated to art and merrymaking is one of the city's tourist hotspots but it has also succeeded in preserving the spirit—at once libertarian and frivolous, rebellious and bohemian—that has made it famous.

The hill was taken over by artists in the 19th century. Géricault, Corot, Renoir, Van Gogh, and Degas were all attracted by the quality of its light, its cheap rents, numerous cabarets, and reputation for loose morals.

Parisians became infatuated with the uninhibited revelry of the Moulin Rouge, where Toulouse-Lautrec sketched his cancan dancers, while the Place Pigalle held its celebrated "models' market," where artists came in search of subjects to paint in the nude. At the dawn of the 20th century crowds flocked to dance the quadrille in the Moulin de la Galette (immortalized by Renoir) or laugh at the witticisms of Aristide Bruant in the Lapin Agile. Van Dongen, Juan Gris,

Vlaminck, Braque, and Picasso got drunk together while discussing art in the Bateau-Lavoir. From the Place des Abbesses to the forecourt of the Sacré-Coeur, steep streets and interminable flights of steps further enhance the special atmosphere of Montmartre and its picturesque lifestyle. The Place du Tertre, the village's legendary square, is well worth the climb as it rewards visitors with a host of restaurants and bistros, as well as street painters eager to sketch them.

The hill is dominated by the brilliant whiteness of the Sacré-Coeur, built as part of a national drive to heal the wounds of political instability, particularly the upheaval of the Paris Commune in 1870. Its domes, bell towers, and Romanic-Byzantine façade overlook an area stretching from the Place Pigalle to the Saint-Vincent cemetery.

Montmartre: Bohemian Playground

Crowds of tourists climb the hill all year round, and even though the confident, creative village has lost a little of its sense of freedom, a visit to its festival marking the grape harvest reveals that the locals retain their spirit of bonhomie and their sense of humor.

[1] According to a lyric written by Jean Renoir for the singer Cora Vaucaire, "The steps of the hill are hard for the destitute."

[2] The terraces of the Jardin du Sacré-Coeur are a perfect place to enjoy the panoramic view of the entire city.

[3] The entrance to Hôtel de Ville Métro station originally belonged to Abbesses station in Montmartre. It was transferred in 1972.
[4] The carousel on Square Willette, renamed Square Louise-Michel in 2004.
[5] The funicular train provides a leisurely alternative to the steps!

[1] Tourists who want to take away a sketched portrait are never disappointed on the Place du Tertre.
[2] Bohemia cannot exist without cafés: *Tartempion* is typical of Montmartre and serves classic French dishes.

[3] The Bateau-Lavoir on Place Émile-Goudeau is just one example of Montmartre's status as an early-twentieth-century powerhouse of artistic innovation. It was in a studio here that Picasso laid the foundations of Cubism by painting *Les Demoiselles d'Avignon* in 1907.

[4] The pink house on Rue des Saules became famous after being featured in a painting by Utrillo.

341

[1] [2] and [right] The climb up 327 steps to the top of the dome in the Sacré-Coeur is rewarded by an unbeatable view of the city.
[3] The basilica's choir was covered with a Byzantine-style mosaic in 1923.

[1] The Élysée Montmartre, which once showcased the cancan, is now a rock music venue.
[2] The Boris Vian Foundation is located at no. 6, Cité Véron.
[3] A heartfelt plea for success in an exam, left by a visitor to the Sacré-Coeur.

[4] The *Moulin de la Galette* restaurant, topped by the Radet mill, was once a dance hall.
[5] The name of the Lapin Agile is a pun on the surname of the painter (Gill) who designed its sign.

Rue Saint-Vincent is the site of one of the best-known vineyards in Paris. Its wine is quite expensive but its profits help fund social institutions. It is overlooked by some attractive buildings dating from the 1930s.

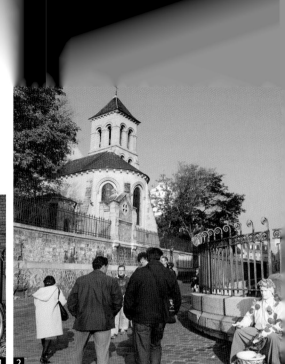

[1] Some hardy spirits tackle the slopes of Montmartre by bike.
[2] The Church of Saint-Pierre de Montmartre, less famous than the neighboring Sacré-Coeur, is one of the oldest in Paris.
[3] The rooftops of Paris in an atmosphere reminiscent of Impressionism.

These neighborhoods are the heart of popular, working-class Paris, spreading along the streets and alleys that tumble down the slopes of this hill in the east of the city.

Édith Piaf, the songstress of street life, was born on Rue de Belleville, while Maurice Chevalier would immortalize his home neighborhood of Ménilmontant with his ebullience and cheeky accent. Colorful shops and exotic restaurants have long since replaced the open-air dancing venues of the 19th century, but their spirit lingers on. The area has never turned its back on its working-class origins and the numerous immigrant communities that form its population today continue to honor the values of solidarity and sharing, while dividing their times between cafés and courtyards.

Everyday life in this neighborhood is found as much in its new planned developments as on its old streets. The modest apartment blocks with small gardens, clustered around a private street, are now typical working-class homes that illustrate the relentless division of property that characterized planning in Belleville from 1840 to the early 20th century. The blocks line the alleys and passageways linking the streets of Belleville and Ménilmontant; they were once paths marking the boundaries of fields full of vines, and Parisians would come here on Sunday to enjoy the local wine, or *guiguet*, and listen to the musette playing. This atmosphere of convivial revelry is still present, as the cafés and restaurants running from the top of Ménilmontant to Oberkampf are now an essential part of Parisian nightlife.

The appearance of the neighborhood is constantly changing, however, and some development and renovation programs have proven unpopular. Gone are the days when Jean-Jacques Rousseau came to collect plants

From Belleville to Ménilmontant: The "Rebellious Children"

in the park of Saint-Fargeau Chateau.The trees of Belleville's cemetery are the only remains of the estate that once dominated this ever-lively village.

[1] Villa Castel, on Rue du Transvaal. Truffaut filmed some scenes from *Jules et Jim* here.
[2] The popular market on the Boulevard de Belleville stretches for hundreds of yards.
[3] House with garden, Rue des Couronnes.

[4] The Passage de la Fonderie on Rue Jean-Pierre-Timbaud, bears witness to the neighborhood's working-class history.
[5] The Maison de l'Air is an educational center seeking to raise awareness about the importance of clean air and controlling pollution.

[1] The former Meccano factory at no. 80, Rue Rebéval.
[2] Colorful, cosmopolitan storefronts on the Boulevard de Belleville.
[3] This street name refers to an Algerian village; it leads to the Rue du Sénégal.

[4] La Bellevilloise, the first working-class cooperative (founded in 1877), is now a hall for events and performances.
[5] Local shops still have a place along the fashionable Rue Oberkampf.
[6] Rue Oberkampf, with its series of cafés and restaurants, has recently become a favorite meeting place for the city's hipsters.

[Right] The Church of Saint-Germain-de-Charonne was the parish church for the old village of Charonne until 1860, when it was annexed by Paris.

[1] Villa Poissonnière, in the Goutte d'Or neighborhood.
[2] Passage Plantin, between Rue des Couronnes and Rue du Transvaal.
[3] Sundial on the Church of Saint-Germain-de-Charonne.

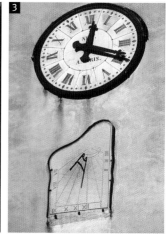

[1] Paths lined with flowers at the foot of the Parc de Belleville. [2] and [3] To the east of Ménilmontant, the Hameau du Danube gives the city a rural touch.

[4] The Rue Dennoyer provides a stage for alternative art.
[5] Villa Castel, far removed from the hub-bub of the city.
[6] A mural by Némo graces the façade of a supermarket on Rue de Ménilmontant.

357

As Victor Hugo wrote in The Hunchback *of Notre Dame*, the Île de la Cité and the Île Saint-Louis were "the head, heart, and essence of Paris."

Despite the tourists that throng the forecourt of Notre Dame Cathedral all year long, the Île de la Cité remains the most mysterious place in Paris, open to all possibilities, both emotional and visual. Not far from the cathedral, the island still preserves some charming oases, such as the flower market on Place Louis-Lépine, where time seems to stand still. The stalls overflowing with camellias, orchids, jasmine, and bamboo complement the carved stone of the Hôtel-Dieu and the Palais de Justice.

The quays lead to the Place Dauphine, which oozes a captivating charm, and, further on past the Pont Neuf, the oldest bridge in Paris, the Square du Vert-Galant on the eastern tip of the island basks in tranquility. Next to the Île de la Cité, the Île Saint-Louis is reached by crossing the bridge of the same name. This island is distinguished by the remarkable architectural homogeneity and splendor of its town houses dating from the 17th century. Among the most opulent examples are the Hôtel de Lauzun, the Hôtel Lambert, and the Hôtel de Richelieu, which were built by Louis Le Vau, the master of French classicism.

Pedestrians rule here as cars have problems getting around. Its central thoroughfare, the Rue Saint-Louis-en-l'Île, is crowned by its Baroque church, with its original openwork belfry and unusual clock. This street also boasts art galleries, small hotels, libraries, and restaurants. The Île Saint-Louis is smaller and undeniably the quieter of the two islands. It exudes an aristocratic village

The Île Saint-Louis and the Île de la Cité: The Heart of the World

atmosphere where even the taste of a Berthillon ice cream can whisk a visitor to another world.

[1] and [4] The terrace of the Berthillon ice-cream parlor—an institution on the Île Saint-Louis.
[3] Every porch on the Quai d'Anjou hides secrets from the past.

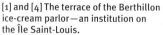

360

[2] and [5] The wharfs on both the islands invite visitors to take a stroll. [6] A detail of the Hôtel Lambert, which was one of Louis Le Vau's earlier buildings.

[Following pages] The flower market on the Île de la Cité is the last of its kind to survive in Paris. On Sundays it is taken over by an animal market.

[1] and [right] The flower market on the Île de la Cité is awash with greenery.
[2] Rue Chanoinesse is the medieval nucleus of the island.
[3] This terrace is ideally positioned close to the tourist sights.

[1] The two houses on the corner of the Place Dauphine were built by Henri IV in 1607 in honor of the Dauphin Louis (later Louis XIII).

[2] and [3] The Church of Saint-Louis-en-l'Île, with its openwork belfry and finely wrought clock.

[4] The terraces on the Place Dauphine are popular with employees of the nearby Palais de Justice.

[5] A stunning view of the Île Saint-Louis and the Marais from the top of Notre Dame.

367

The Rue Mouffetard is a lively,
cosmopolitan street running
through the Latin Quarter.

Visitors are delighted and exhilarated by the spirit of the Left Bank: from the Place de Fürstenberg to the Sorbonne, from the Church of Saint-Germain-des-Prés to the Panthéon, from the School of Medicine to the arenas of Lutetia, from the Place de la Contrescarpe to the Church of Saint-Séverin.

More than any sense of history, it is an intoxicating art of living that permeates the medieval streets and student squares, the café terraces and legendary stores. The two neighborhoods separated by the Boulevard Saint-Michel are distinguished by an intellectual outreach that has never waned. After eight centuries as an academic powerhouse, the Latin Quarter maintains its intellectual traditions through dozens of schools dotted round the Sorbonne. On the Rue de la Huchette and the Rue Mouffetard, tourists and students cross paths in a maze of picturesque streets that now play host to Greek restaurants and off-the-rack retail stores. The old spirit lives on, however, and the streets offer a constant spectacle.

After World War II, the neighborhood of Saint-Germain-des-Prés became a cultural and intellectual hub. Actors, writers, philosophers, poets, and publishers rubbed shoulders to the sound of the jazz emanating from the cellars where Boris Vian held court. Jean-Paul Sartre and Simone de Beauvoir expounded their ideas in the *Deux Magots*, the *Flore*, and the *Lipp* brasserie, leaving behind the mark of their existentialist philosophy, just as Giacometti, Jacques Prévert, François Truffaut, and Juliette Gréco have left their artistic stamp on the entire neighborhood.

From Saint-Germain-des-Prés to the Latin Quarter: The Spirit of the Left Bank

While the modern galleries and bookstores now co-exist with up-market stores, the romantic colors of this neighborhood are still impregnated with a subtle mixture of tradition, creativity, and frivolity.

[1] The sign for the Nègre Joyeux (no. 14, Rue Mouffetard) shows Madame du Barry with her black page.
[2] Fountain on Rue de Bazeilles, at the bottom of Rue Mouffetard.
[3] Bookstores and antiquarian book dealers thrive in Saint-Germain-des-Prés, the quintessential intellectual neighborhood.

LIVRES RARES

The cultures and flavors of the world are on display on the "Mouff," the street with a thousand faces.

[1] and [3] Rue Mouffetard is an old, picturesque street that has preserved its strikingly playful signs.
[2] A philosophical mural by Pierre Alechinsky alongside a poem by Yves Bonnefoy decorates the side of a building on Rue Descartes, right next to Rue Mouffetard.

[4] The terraces on the Place Saint-André-des-Arts have replaced a church knocked down after the Revolution.
[5] The façade of no. 134, Rue Mouffetard is classified as a historic monument.

[1] Shakespeare & Company, the Latin Quarter's legendary English-language bookstore.

[2] [4] and [5] Graffiti on the passages in the Monge neighborhood and memories of the Paris of yesteryear in a shop window… everything is possible on Rue Mouffetard!

[3] Haussmann cut off the southern part of Rue Mouffetard in order to construct the Avenue des Gobelins.

[6] Picasso's sculpture of Dora Maar stands on the Square Laurent Prache, at the foot of Saint-Germain-des-Prés.

The village origins of La Butte-aux-Cailles have been entirely obscured by the transformations that have taken place over time. The distinctive soil composition of its underground lime quarries have afforded it protection, ruling out the construction of any heavy buildings (in contrast to the nearby Place d'Italie, now studded with skyscrapers).

The neighborhood is centered on the area between Rue de la Butte-aux-Cailles and Rue des Cinq-Diamants; beyond this, small narrow streets and paved passages offer a delightful promenade seemingly caught in the past. In the courtyard of an old farm, redbrick terraced houses with discreet half-timbering make up what is known as "Little Alsace." This public housing from the 1910s adjoins the Villa Daviel, tucked into

La Butte-aux-Cailles: A Breath of Freedom

a typically Parisian private road, lined with elegantly uniform houses and charming, well-kept gardens. A little further on, the gardens around the terraced houses in the Cité Florale are maintained with the same loving care; here the street names add a touch of poetry, as they evoke flowers such as orchids, wisteria, and morning-glory.

An aquifer made it possible to build a swimming pool in La Butte-aux-Cailles way back in 1924. It is not only one of the oldest pools in Paris; it is also unusual because it is supplied with ferruginous water at a temperature of 82.4°F (28°C) by an artesian well 1,916 ft. (584 m) deep. The village's nightlife is enriched by its array of cafés and restaurants. Although the partying can go on rather too late for some locals, the atmosphere is laid-back. The independent, libertarian spirit prevalent at the time of the Commune still resonates today in cooperative café-restaurants that perpetuate this tradition of self-determination.

The names Rue des Orchidées, Rue des Iris, and the Rue des Volubilis exemplify the flowery language of the Cité Florale (13th arrondissement).

This unexpected village, miraculously saved from the property developers by its fragile subsoil, creates a rural atmosphere in the midst of the city.

[1] and [2] Rue Buot and Passage Boiton. These streets slope down to converge in the center of La Butte-aux-Cailles. [3] and [5] Houses with a regular gabled formation on Rue Henri Pape and Rue Dieulafoy.

380

[4] "Little Alsace" consists of some thirty terraced houses with half-timbering. They form a public housing project dating from the 1910s.

[1] The Art Deco swimming pool of La Butte-aux-Cailles (1924) is sheltered by a reinforced concrete vault.
[2] and [3] Urban expression forms part of the scenery.

[4] and [5] The Merle Moqueur ("Mocking Blackbird") has long been a fixture of La Butte's nightlife.
[6] The headquarters of the Amis de la Commune (Friends of the Commune), at no. 46, Rue des Cinq-Diamants.

383

The bohemian spirit that infused Montparnasse in the early 20ᵗʰ century has long been extinguished. The sumptuous parties and the creative outpourings on café terraces and in artists' studios are now merely memories that linger over the few places that have survived the almost total transformation of this key element in the city's history.

Artists of the stature of Léger, Chagall, and Zadkine called Montparnasse home, while Picasso, Modigliani, Blaise Cendrars, and countless others gathered in the *Rotonde* and the *Dôme*, and Paul Fort and later Ernest Hemingway found inspiration in the *Closerie des Lilas*. Montparnasse reached its apogee in the crazy years of the 1920s, when artists mingled with socialites to a soundtrack of jazz in bars such as the *Sélect*, the first to stay open all night.

The Carrefour Vavin, graced by Rodin's statue of Balzac, was the hub of postwar Parisian life, but these days visitors must explore the

Montparnasse: The Crazy Years

Modern buildings like the railroad station and the Maine-Montpar-nasse Tower have replaced the small streets lined with low-rent houses that once acted as a magnet for artists. Painters, sculptors, and poets from all over the world settled here and made it an international showcase for modern art. The sculptor Alfred Boucher salvaged a polygonal pavilion built by Eiffel from the 1900 Universal Exhibition to create an artists' village, La Ruche, which can still be seen today.

side-streets off the main boulevards to find village life (albeit in a somewhat watered-down form). There are still plenty of artists' studios but they are now overshadowed by the hubbub of modern life. Nevertheless, the Rue Daguerres, the studios on the Square Montsouris, and the market on Boulevard Edgar Quinet bear witness to a lifestyle that continues to endure in Montparnasse.

[2] Montparnasse station, which serves all the western part of France, has attracted a significant Breton community—and their typical *crêperies*.

[1] [4] and [5] The Rue de la Gaîté was dotted with meeting places that smuggled wine past the Denfert-Rochereau tollhouse. It still boasts many bars and theaters.

[3] La Ruche became an artists' community in 1902. It contained 140 low-rent studios and its tenants included Chagall, Soutine, and Léger.

[1] The sign of the Paris Accordéon on the Rue Daguerre.
[2] [3] and [5] Picasso, Aragon, and Faulkner still haunt the walls of Montparnasse's mythical bars: The *Rotonde*, the *Sélect* and the *Dôme*.
[4] Rodin's *Balzac* stands tall above the Carrefour Vavin.

5

6

[6] The genuine spirit of village Paris: the Rue Daguerre, with its stalls selling fruit, vegetables, fish, and cheese.

[1] The Villa d'Alésia is sheltered from the bustle of the city.
[2] and [6] Well-concealed havens of peace behind the Rue Didot: the Villas Jamot, Collet, Deshaye.
[3] The house-studio of the painter Amédée Ozenfant, built by Le Corbusier on Avenue Reille.

[4] Although the Square Montsouris and its Art Deco houses are private property, it is open to pedestrians.

[5] The houses on the Passage d'Enfer, which retains the former name of the Boulevard Raspail.
[7] Rue Georges-Braque is named for the painter who commissioned Auguste Perret to build a house at no. 6.

Modern
Paris

The second half of the 20th century was marked in Paris by a striving for modernity, opening up new horizons, and achieving prestige through architecture. It reached to the skies in response to the city's demographic and economic expansion.

Development in the neighborhood of La Défense, Europe's first business district, was begun in the 1950s. It lies at the end of the majestic Grand Axis, the visionary thoroughfare running from the Arc de Triomphe du Carrousel through the Étoile, and now culminating in the fabulous, ground-breaking cube of La Défense. The quays on the Seine from the Pont Mirabeau to the Champ-de-Mars have also had a facelift. This neighborhood, once inhabited by workers from nearby factories, has undergone a major renovation program involving the construction of twenty high-rise blocks, combining both residential and tertiary sector use.

The 13th arrondissement has similarly been transformed by the addition of over thirty blocks more than 330 ft. (100 m) high, grouped around the entrance to the Olympiades Métro station. The Far Eastern refugees that arrived in Paris en masse in the 1970s soon settled in this neighborhood, earning it the title of "Chinatown." Paris is in a constant state of flux, but the overhaul of Les Halles, the erstwhile "stomach" of the city so vividly described by Zola, constituted the most radical rupture with its past to date. Baltard's covered market, for so long the lifeblood of Paris, was moved to Rungis, to be replaced by an underground shopping mall, a train station, and a park.

The Trailblazers of Today's Paris

Henceforward, the neighborhood would feed the spirit, extending the realm of culture from Les Halles to the gates of the Marais (where the Pompidou Center had just opened), from the maze of the medieval streets to the stone buildings lining Haussmann's boulevards.

[1] and [2] Place René-Cassin, the Stock Exchange, and Henri de Miller's *L'Écoute* in the gardens of Les Halles.
[3] The Forum des Halles, one of the first major redevelopment projects in central Paris, provides plenty of work for window cleaners!

The five-story Forum, perfectly integrated into the hole left by the covered market, was drawn up by the architects Vasconi and Penchréach in 1979. It is due to be modernized in the near future.

[Following pages] Contrasts of lines and materials above the Porte du Jour.

397

[1] Montparnasse station was refurbished in 1987 to accommodate the TGV-Atlantique high-speed train service.
[2] The Jardin Atlantique, opened in 1994, has been laid out above the station.
[3] At the time of its construction in 1972, the Maine-Montparnasse Tower was the highest office block in Europe (689 ft./210 m).

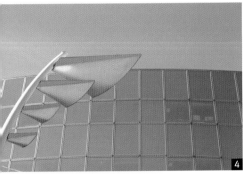

4 **5**

6

[4] The masts designed by the sculptor Bernard Vié serve to reflect sunlight into shady areas. [5] and [6] The Jardin Atlantique is spread over 8½ acres (3.5 hectares), the same size as the Place de la Concorde. Its greenery comprises plants from France's western regions that are capable of growing in less than 12 in. (30 cm) of soil.

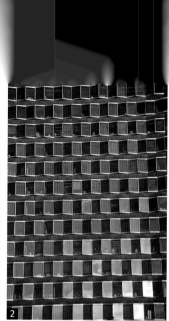

[1] The Radio France building was opened in 1963 and superbly renovated in 2008. [2] and [3] The twenty towers on the bank of the Seine (15th arrondissement) soar to heights of over 330 ft. (100 m).

[4] The Crystal Tower was the last to be completed (1990).
[5] The replica of the Statue of Liberty was donated by French immigrants in the United States to mark the centenary of the Revolution. It was put in place in 1889 but was turned westward in 1937 to face its counterpart in New York.

[Following pages] The twenty towers on the bank of the Seine have been altered several times since the 1960s; the most recent modernization program began in 2008.

Operation Italie XIII
was launched in the
1960s to endow the
13th arrondissement
with revolutionary
skyscrapers.
It was interrupted
in the 1970s.

[1] Tour Super-Italie, on Avenue d'Italie.
[2] Tour Chambord, on Boulevard Kellerman.

[Left] The 3 ½ million sq. yards (3 million sq. m) of office space in La Défense, Europe's foremost business district, provide employment for 150,000 people.

[Following pages] More than 1,500 firms operate behind the glass façades of La Défense.

[1] The towers are reflected in a pool on the esplanade designed by the artist Takis, who embellished it with forty-nine "luminous trees."

[2] The Coeur Défense Building, completed in 2001, boasts the most usable floor space in Europe. Its two main towers are 528 ft. (161 m) high and are rounded at each end.

[3] The barges anchored on the wharfs of Neuilly have an exceptional view of the tower blocks.

[1] Raymond Moretti's *Chimney*, 105 ft. (32 m) high, is made up of colored tubes.
[2] Monumental fountain designed by Yaacov Agam.
[3] The fountain on the Pont de Neuilly leading toward the Great Arch.
[4] A little vegetation amid the towers.

5 **6**

7

[5] The Boulevard Circulaire, skirting La Défense.
[6] The natural scenery at the tip of the Île de la Jatte lies close to the towers.
[7] The forecourt of La Défense, with the Great Arch and the CNIT (Center for New Industries and Technologies).

413

[1] View from the banks of the Seine in Neuilly.
[2] The Areva Tower (604 ft./184 m) is the second highest block in La Défense, after the Total Tower (613 ft./187 m).

[3] The Coeur Défense Tower, built in 2001.
[4] The AXA Tower was put up in 1974 and refurbished in 2008.

The structures and layout of Paris that were in place prior to its modern era have been enhanced by spectacular buildings designed by some of the greatest names in modern architecture. The city's unique architectural and planning heritage lives alongside—and sometimes in opposition to—a new vision of Paris.

"palace of popular culture." The Pompidou Center (Beaubourg Centre Georges Pompidou), with its entrails on view in a colorful casing and steel tubes exposed outside, sparked strong reactions, although it has now blended into the scenery of Paris.

The major architectural projects instigated by President François Mitterand have confirmed the mastery of both renowned French architects like Jean Nouvel, author of the Arab World Institute, and foreigners, as in the joint work of the native Paul Chemetov and the Chilean Borja Huidobro, responsible for the Ministry of Finance.

The influence of Le Corbusier can be felt in the residential towers of the 13th or 19th arrondissements, but their functionality, homogeneity, and alignment lack a human touch. Many felt that 20th-century architecture should address this deficiency by expressing the spirit of the future, and in 1969, President Georges Pompidou took the initiative by asking Renzo Piano and Richard Rogers to build a new

From Le Corbusier to Jean Nouvel

The glass-and-metal pyramid built by the Chinese-American Ieoh Ming Pei in the middle of the Louvre's Cour Napoléon continues to arouse controversy among some critics but the public embraced it from the start. The same was true of the Tolbiac by Dominique Perrautt.

416

[1] and [2] The Pompidou Center, designed by Renzo Piano and Richard Rogers, was vilified in 1971 but it is now the city's third most visited monument.
[3] The tubes of the Pompidou Center, visible from the Rue du Renard, received fierce criticism but are now an integral part of the neighborhood's identity.

[4] The IRCAM building was also conceived by Renzo Piano and Richard Rogers (in 1990).
[5] The Fontaine Stravinsky pays homage to the art of music through movement.

[3] The Cité de la Musique, the work of Christian de Portzamparc, was the last element of the Parc de la Villette to be completed (1995).

[1] The Grande Halle market in La Villette, once a slaughterhouse, was refurbished in 1985 by the architects Bernard Reichen and Philippe Robert. [2] The Cité des Sciences et de l'Industrie, built by Adrien Fainsilber, was opened in 1986.

[4] The Grande Halle, built in 1867, is as fine example of the period's metal architecture. It was renovated in 2007. [5] The Cité des Sciences et de l'Industrie welcomes over 3 million visitors every year.

The Cité des Sciences combines three elements: water, light, and vegetation.

[Right] The *Géode*, built by the architect Adrien Fainsilber and the engineer Gérard Chamayou, was opened on May 6, 1985. It is equipped with an 85-ft. (26-m) hemispherical screen.

[1] and [2] The Musée du Quai Branly, designed by Jean Nouvel, is the most recent of the great Parisian museums. It opened in 2006.
[3] Quai Branly, adorned with one of Patrick Blanc's vertical gardens.

[4] The *Kiosque des Noctambules* is a new Métro entrance on Place Colette. It was built in 2000 by Jean-Michel Othoniel for the centenary of the Parisian subway system.

[5] The *Heure de Tous* by Arman, erected in front of Saint-Lazare station (1985).

[6] Daniel Buren's notorious columns in the Palais-Royal, installed in 1985.

[1] The Arab World Institute, which opened in 1981, was jointly designed by Jean Nouvel and the Architecture Studio. It was intended to encourage exchange between Arab and European cultures. Its facilities include a museum and art galleries...

...as well as an auditorium and a panoramic restaurant.
[2] The institute's windows, which resemble a *moucharaby*, open and close via a system of diaphragms controlled by the exterior light.

[3] and [5] Rue Mallet-Stevens, created in 1927, is a showcase for the legacy of the eponymous architect, a leading light of Art Deco. Several private houses, including no. 10, home of his offices, are emblematic of this contemporary art movement.

[4] The Le Corbusier Foundation, established in accordance with the architect's wishes, is situated on the Square du Dr-Blanche in twin villas called La Roche and Jeanneret (Le Corbusier's real surname).

The Place de Séoul (14th arrondissement), with its gigantic glass-fronted rotunda, was built by Ricardo Bofill. It still arouses controversy today.

[1] Shamaï Haber's fountain in the middle of Bofill's Place de Catalogne (14th arrondissement) is a huge sloping granite disk with water trickling down it.
[2] In 1965 Oscar Niemeyer donated his services to the French Communist Party to design its headquarters on the Place du Colonel-Fabien.

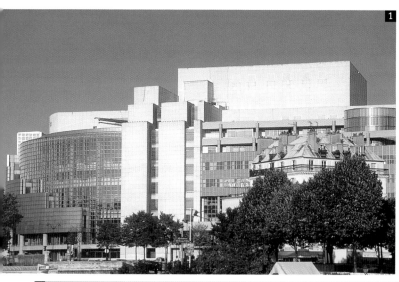

[1] The Opéra Bastille was designed by Carlos Ott. It opened in 1989 to celebrate the 200th anniversary of the storming of the Bastille.

[2] The Ministry of the Economy and Finances was drawn up by the architects Paul Chemetov and Borja Huidobro in 1989. It includes two arches, 236 ft. (72 m) wide; one stretches into the Seine, above the Quai de Bercy, the other passes over the Rue de Bercy.

The Cinémathèque Française, adapted by Dominique Brad from an initial project by Frank Gehry, has moved from Chaillot to the Parc de Bercy.

431

3 [1] and [2] The "Paris, Rive Gauche" neighborhood, built around the François Mitterrand Library, was conceived by top architects and constitutes the biggest change in the Parisian landscape since the 1970s.
[3] The Josephine Baker swimming pool is anchored off the Quai Mauriac. Its steel-and-glass structure, the work of the architect Robert de Busni, is kept afloat by twenty metal supports.

[4] Dominique Perrault conceived the Mitterrand Library as four open books.
[5] The Simone de Beauvoir pedestrian bridge, the thirty-seventh bridge on the Seine, was built by Dietmar Feichtinger. It has linked the Parc de Bercy with the BNF neighborhood since 2006.

In 2006 the Maréchaux light rail line transformed the landscape and communications between the Porte d'Ivry and the Pont de Garigliano.

The city's first Métro line was opened between Vincennes and Maillot in 1900 for the Universal Exhibition. Since then it has carried countless foreign tourists and even more Parisians intent on coming and going with efficiency.

Paris has also witnessed the evolution of public transport; from horse-drawn vehicles in 1828 through a series of technological developments that brought with them steam power, compressed air, and the jet engine. It was only in 1973, with the introduction of the ring road, that Paris attempted to implement traffic control.

Four years later, the RER station in Châtelet-les-Halles became the largest underground train station in the world and improved access to the entire Paris region.

The streetcar, long neglected because it was considered incompatible with the automobile, made a comeback in 2006 on the Boulevard Maréchaux-Sud. Paris is trying to breathe again, because the political will to combat the pollution created by automobiles is now much stronger, and Parisians are rediscovering the long-lost pleasure of walking on pedestrian streets. The roads running along the riverbanks, classified as a world heritage site by UNESCO, are closed to traffic on Sundays and public holidays, when they play host to an array of social and leisure activities.

In 2007, the bicycle finally came into its own as a means of transport via the introduction of the Vélib service. Every Friday evening, crowds of rollerbladers glide freely through the streets of Paris in a party atmosphere—evidence of its citizens' very human desire to stamp their personality on

Paris in Motion

their habitat. The famous Paris Marathon has passed through several neighborhoods since 1976, to great popular acclaim, while various parts of the capital are endowed with sports stadiums, such as the Parc des Princes, the Stade Charléty, and the Stade de France.

[1] The Olympiades Métro station, the southern terminus of line 14, became the most recent addition to the subway system in 2007.

[2] The Vélib, a self-service bicycle rental scheme launched in 2007, has proved a huge success.

[3] Open-air double-decker buses will never go out of fashion with tourists!

[4] The roads along the riverbanks are closed to cars on Sunday—much to the delight of rollerbladers.

[5] The pace of the Paris Marathon leaves runners little time to observe the scenery.

[1] Nine hippodromes are situated in the suburbs of Paris. Seen here, the prestigious Prix d'Amérique in the Vincennes hippodrome.
[2] The Poterne des Peupliers light rail station. Streetcars were last seen in Paris in 1938.
[3] The Quai des Tuileries jammed with cars.

438

[4] Line 6 of the Métro is among the most appreciated by both tourists and Parisians. When it goes above ground, it offers unique views of various monuments.

[5] Demonstration by campaigners for the "horse in Paris."

Apart from its theaters and opera houses, Paris also boasts many cabaret and concert venues:
[1] Cabaret Sauvage in La Villette
[2] The Balajo, Rue de Lappe
[3] The Zénith
[4] The Cigale, Boulevard de Rochechouart.

[5] The Divan du Monde, Rue des Martyrs
[6] The Trianon, Boulevard de Rochechouart
[7] The Folies Pigalle, Place Pigalle.

You can do anything in Paris — even go ice-skating every winter at the foot of the Maine-Montparnasse Tower or in front of the City Hall.

[1] Standing above the beltway, the Parc des Princes, built in 1972 by the architect Roger Taillibert, has been the home ground for the Paris Saint-Germain soccer club since 1974.
[2] The Paris-Bercy stadium puts on both sporting events and major concerts.

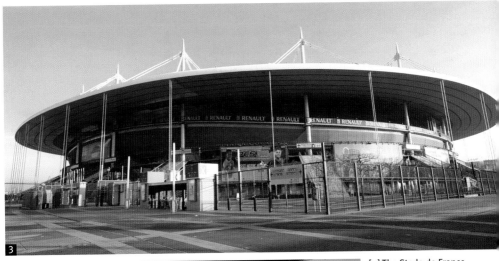

[3] The Stade de France was opened in 1998 for the soccer World Cup. It also plays host to numerous sports events, concerts, and large-scale spectacles.
[4] The Charléty stadium, designed by the architect Henri Gaudin, is a large complex used for various sports, most particularly athletics.

445

Paris has long been regarded as the capital of fashion, luxury, and *haute couture*, from the extravagant outfits of Marie-Antoinette to Coco Chanel's little black dress, from the courtesans of the Second Empire to the top models of today.

In the Second Empire, rich sophisticates swelled the clientele of the jewelers who had moved from the Palais-Royal to the Rue de la Paix and the Place Vendôme, where the luxury suites of the recently opened Ritz Hotel became the favored port-of-call of high society. The Lutetia Hotel, in the heart of Saint-Germain-des-Prés, was specially built to accommodate customers from the Bon Marché, the city's first department store—an art deco masterpiece devoted to luxury and enticement that served as inspiration for Zola in his novel *Au Bonheur des Dames*.

Two subsequent department stores, Le Printemps and the Galeries Lafayette on Boulevard Haussmann, have now become tourist sights in their own right, just as much as any of the city's great monuments. Fashion houses such as Dior, Chanel, Ungaro, and Lanvin, situated in the so-called "golden triangle" extending from the Avenue Montaigne to the Faubourg Saint-Honoré, represent a long tradition of skill and talent that has brought them fame and fortune. The Place des Victoires is another fashion mecca, while the Colette boutique on Rue Saint-Honoré has become a shopping temple that can establish or destroy trends overnight via its storefront displays and choice of accessories.

Fashion, Luxury, and Design

Although Milan, London, and New York quickly caught up with Paris in terms of creativity, the French capital can draw on a tradition of unequalled artistry passed on from one generation to the next. Furthermore, the Parisian woman still embodies style, freedom, and romance in the popular imagination.

[1] and [4] The department stores on the main boulevards try to outdo each other's decorative lighting effects at Christmastime.

[2] [3] and [5] The Champs-Élysées is synonymous for luxury and pleasure the whole world over.

449

[1] [2] and [3] Rue du Faubourg-Saint-Honoré is dotted with the top names of the fashion world.
[4] and [right] Hédiard and Fauchon, or the delicatessen as fine art.

[1] Village Royal is a peaceful area close to the Madeleine Church that specializes in famous brand names.
[2] Caviar Kaspia, the epitome of luxury and refinement, takes pride of place on the Place de la Madeleine.
[3] Many major brands have outlets between the great boulevards and the Opera House.

[4] and [6] Vintage houses rub shoulders with fashion designers in a culture of elegance and luxury on Avenue George-V. [5] Bercy Village has metamorphosed from a center of the wine industry into a fashionable shopping district.

The luxury hotels of Paris are the stuff of dreams, except for a select few: [1] and [2] The Fouquet's Barrière and the Hôtel Marriott on the Champs-Élysées. [3] The Prince de Galles, on Avenue George-V.

[4] Bon Marché, the first of the department stores.
[5] [6] and [7] Cartier, Vuitton, Saint-Laurent: these names are evocative of Paris in all four corners of the globe.

[1] and [3] Multi-nationals can now be found alongside the traditional names on the Avenue des Champs-Élysées.
[2] The famous Hermès HQ at no. 24, Rue du Faubourg-Saint-Honoré.

[4] The Hotel George V is a monument to Art Deco.
[5] The Lutetia, at no. 45, Boulevard Raspail, is the only luxury hotel from the early 20th century to be situated on the Left Bank.

Index

A

Acacias, Passage des 264
Alésia, Villa d' 390
Alexandre III, Pont 126, 170,
   183–185
Alma, Pont de l' 156, 170, 188
Ancre, Passage de l' 236, 242
André-Citroën, Parc 322, 330
Anjou, Quai d' 65, 68, 164,
   358, 360
Arab World Institute (Institut
   du Monde Arabe) 416,
Arc de Triomphe 40, 124, 394
Arc de Triomphe du Carrousel
   40, 306, 314, 394
Archevêché, Pont de l' 175
Architectural Models Museum
   43
Arcole, Pont d' 174
Army Museum 43–44
Arsenal, Jardin de l' 326

Arsenal, Pavillon de l' 58
Arsenal, Port de l' 194, 204,
   205
Artillery Museum 43
Arts, Pont des 79, 85, 156,
   160, 165, 170, 180
Austerlitz, Pont d' 174

B

Bagatelle, Parc de 286, 326
Bastille, Place de la 98, 118,
   182, 204, 326
Bateau-Lavoir 336, 341
Batignolles, Square des 322,
   329
Beaujolais, Passage 250
Beauséjour, Villa 230
Belleville, Parc de 322, 348, 356
Bercy 158, 430, 453
Bercy, Parc de 332, 333, 431,
   433

Billettes, Des (cloister) 29
Bir-Hakeim, Pont 190–191
Bofinger 70, 98, 99
Bon Marché 446, 455
Boulogne, Bois de 286, 288
Bourse du Commerce 57, 396
Brady, Passage 224, 230, 232
Branly, Musée du Quai 416,
   422
Buttes-aux-Cailles 221, 376,
   380, 382, 383
Buttes-Chaumont, Parc des
   294, 296, 297, 298

C

Caire, Passage du 248
Carnavalet, Musée 10, 86
Carrousel, Pont du 170
Castel Béranger 144
Catacombs 268, 270, 274
Catalogne, Place de 429

Chaillot, Théâtre de 131
Champ-de-Mars 49, 126, 129, 131, 301, 394
Champs-Élysées, Avenue des 106, 109, 116, 123, 306, 324, 448, 456
Champs-Élysées, Théâtre des 109
Change, Pont au 30
Charles-de-Gaulle, Place 124
Charléty, Stade 434, 445
Châtelet, Fontaine du 209
Châtelet, Place du 121, 206
Châtelet, Avenue du 121
Choiseul, Passage 251, 255
Cinémathèque Française 431
Cirque d'Hiver 108
Cité de la Musique 420
Cité des Sciences et de l'Industrie 420, 421, 422
Cité Florale 376, 378

Cité, Île de la 110, 156, 170, 172, 174, 324, 358, 361, 364
Clisson, Hôtel de 15
Closerie des Lilas 94, 384
Cluny, Hôtel de 8, 13
Cluny thermal baths 8, 11
Colbert, Galerie 236, 246
Collège de France 77
Comédie-Française 70, 306
Conciergerie 30, 34, 35
Concorde, Place de la 110, 115, 116, 121, 156, 158, 159, 206, 401
Concorde, Pont de la 182
Contrescarpe, Place de la 208, 213, 368
Coupole 70, 96, 97
Croix du Tahoir, Fontaine de la 219
Culture, Ministry of 55
Cuvier, Fontaine 206, 212

D
Dauphine, Place 110, 112, 358, 366, 367
Défense, La 394, 408, 409, 413, 414
Dejazet, Avenue 108
Denfert-Rochereau 122, 268, 270, 387
Deux Magots 70, 94, 368
Dôme 70, 384, 389
Donon, Hôtel 62

[p. 460]

E
Eiffel, Gustave 126, 128, 129, 384
Eiffel Tower 126, 128, 129, 131, 160
Enfer, Passage d' 391
Étoile, Place de l' 110, 124

Europe, Avenue de l' 108

F
Fauchon 450
Félix Potin 149
Fellah, Fontaine du 229
Finance, Ministry of 416, 428
Fine Arts, School of 77
Flamel, Nicolas 36
Fleury, Hôtel de 73
Flore 70, 94, 368
Folies-Bergère 70, 106
Forney Library12
Fouquet's Barrière 454
France, Stade de 434, 445
Front de Seine 402, 403

G
Galeries Lafayette 446
Gare d'Austerlitz 138, 172
Gare de l'Est 140, 141

Gare de Lyon 139, 172
Gare du Nord 139
Gare Montparnasse 386, 400
Gare Saint-Lazare 138
Géode 422
Georges-Brassens, Parc 256, 267, 322, 328
Gobelins 59
Grand Cerf, Passage du 253
Grande Arche de la Défense 40, 394, 412, 413
Grand-Palais 126, 136
Grands Boulevards 236, 448, 452
Grenelle, Pont de 170
Grévin, Musée 252
Guimet, Musée 90

H
Halles, Les 268, 394
Halles, Forum des 396, 397

Hameau Boileau 241
Haussmann 110, 212, 218, 294, 300, 374, 446
Hôtel de Ville (City Hall) 40, 53, 442

I
Iéna, Pont d' 156, 188
Innocents, Fontaine des 217
Institut de France 79, 170, 461, 426
Invalides 40, 42, 44
Invalides, Pont des 136, 188

J
Jardin Atlantique 400, 401
Jardin des Plantes 206, 306, 318
Jarente, Fontaine de 215
Jean-sans-Peur Tower 8, 15
Jouffroy, Passage 236, 252

Julien 70, 100, 101, 265
Justice, Ministry of 68

L
Lambert, Hôtel 65, 68, 358, 361
Lapin Agile 336, 345
Latin Quarter 8, 309, 368, 374
Le Corbusier 390, 416, 427
Library of the History of Paris 68
Lido 106
Lipp (Brasserie) 94, 368
Louis-Philippe, Pont 170, 172
Louvre 8, 40, 79, 82, 84, 85, 156, 165, 170, 180, 315, 416
Lutetia arenas 10, 368
Lutétia, Hôtel 446, 457
Luxembourg Gardens 206, 306, 308, 309, 310, 311, 314

M
Madeleine Church 49, 452
Maine-Montparnasse Tower 274, 384, 400, 442
Maison de la Radio 402
Marais 39, 68, 172, 215, 367, 394
Marie de Médicis, Fontaine 308, 311
Marie, Pont 170, 173
Mars, Fontaine de 219
Matignon, Hôtel 66
Maxim's 126, 150-153
Medicine, School of 74, 76, 368
Ménilmontant 224, 348, 356, 357
Mers, Fontaine des 206
Military School 49, 131
Mirabeau, Pont 170, 192, 193, 394

Molière, Fontaine 218
Monceau, Parc 294, 304, 305
Montmartre 259, 297, 328, 336, 341, 347
Montparnasse 70, 94, 96
Montparnasse Cemetery 268, 274, 275, 276
Montsouris, Parc 294, 298, 300
Montsouris, Square 384, 391
Morris columns 142
Mosque 227
Mouffetard, Rue 368, 370, 371, 372, 373, 374
Moulin-Rouge 70, 107
Museum of Modern Art 93

N
Nation, Place de la 110, 117, 118

National Library (Bibliothèque Nationale) 70, 265, 322, 416, 432, 433
Notre Dame Cathedral 8, 16–23, 25, 172, 175, 260, 358, 367

O
Olympia 107, 126
Opéra Bastille 430
Opéra Garnier 104, 105, 236
Orsay, Musée d' 70, 87, 88, 89, 156
Ourcq, Canal de l' 194, 202, 206

P-Q
Palace of Justice 53, 358
Palais-Bourbon 52
Palais Brogniart 56
Paris-Bercy Stadium 444

Palais-Royal 40, 54, 217, 236, 306, 320, 321, 425, 446
Panoramas, Passage des 236, 252
Panthéon 40, 46, 47, 75, 215, 309, 368
Parc des Princes, 434, 444
Paris Plage 156, 168-169
Passy Viaduct 130
Père-Lachaise Cemetery 268, 278, 280, 282
Petit Palais 126, 137
Picasso Museum 90, 256
Polytechnic School 74
Pompidou Center 394, 416, 418
Pont au Double 175
Pont Neuf 156, 161, 165, 170, 176-179, 181
Printemps, Le 446
Quatre Parties du Monde, Fontaine des 206, 210

Quatre Saisons, Fontaine des 206, 212, 215

R
Ranelagh, Avenue du 109
Renaissance, Avenue de la 109
République, Place de la 119, 215, 236
Rex 106
Ritz Hotel 446
Rivoli, Rue de 121, 258
Rodin Museum 90, 316
Rotonde 384, 389
Rouelle, Pont 190

S
Sacré-Cœur 297, 336, 338, 342, 344, 347
Sainte-Chapelle 8, 26, 28, 29, 53

Saint-Étienne-du-Mont Church 48
Saint-Eustache Church 25
Saint-Germain-l'Auxerrois Church 24
Saint-Germain-des-Prés 29, 368, 370, 375, 446
Saint-Jacques Tower 15
Saint-Louis, Île 358, 360, 367
Saint-Martin Canal 194, 196-197, 199, 200, 204, 267
Saint-Michel, Fontaine 218
Saint-Séverin Church 48, 368
Saint-Sulpice Church 48
Salé, Hôtel 70, 90, 256, 261, 264
Seine 8, 126, 129, 156, 166, 168, 170, 188, 194, 204, 394, 414, 430
Sélect, Le 384, 389
Senate 306

Sens, Hôtel de 8, 12
Simone-de-Beauvoir pedestrian bridge 433
Sorbonne 40, 70, 72, 368
Soubise, Hôtel de 40, 60, 64
Stalingrad, Place de 194
Stravinsky, Fontaine 206, 419

T
Tertre, Place du 336, 340
Théâtre de la Ville 121
Tokyo Palace 92
Tour d'Argent, la 70, 95
Tournelle, Pont de la 172
Trocadéro 126, 131, 134, 135
Tuileries 306, 314, 315, 316

V
Vélib 436
Vendôme, Place 68, 110, 114, 446

Verdeau, Galerie 236
Verdeau, Passage 254
Vert-Galant, Square du 16, 324, 331
Viaduc des Arts 325
Victoires, Place des 110, 114, 446
Villette, Bassin de la 194, 202
Villette, Grande Halle de la 420, 421
Villette, La 215, 440
Villette, Parc de la 420
Vincennes Chateau 8, 30
Vivienne, Galerie 236, 246, 247
Vosges, Place des 110, 112, 113

W-Z
Wallace Fountains 221
Zénith 440

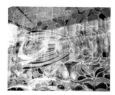

[1001 photographs]